BRINGING JUSTICE TO THE PEOPLE

Bringing Justice to the People

THE STORY OF THE FREEDOM-BASED PUBLIC INTEREST LAW MOVEMENT

Edited by Lee Edwards

Foreword by Edwin Meese III

Published by Heritage Books
an activity of The Heritage Foundation
214 Massachusetts Avenue, NE
Washington, DC 20002–4999
202-546-4400 • heritage.org

Library of Congress Control Number:
2004110147

Printed in the United States of America

Distributed to the trade by
National Book Network
Lanham, Maryland

ISBN 0-9743665-2-8 (Cloth)

Book and cover design by Camille Culbertson
© 2004 by The Heritage Foundation

TABLE OF CONTENTS

Foreword

Edwin Meese III

The individuals and institutions that make up the freedom-based public interest law movement can be justly proud of what they have accomplished in the past 30 years. The pages of this history record their significant legal victories in such critical areas as property rights, school choice, religious freedom, eliminating racial discrimination, freedom of speech, workers' rights, and economic liberty.

The guiding principle of this movement has been ordered liberty—the prudential blending of individual freedom and political order. Its guiding document is the U.S. Constitution. Its jurisprudence is a Jurisprudence of Original Intention, by which its lawyers seek to judge policies in light of principles rather than to remold principles to fit policy, as too many of today's liberals are wont to do. The objective of this legal movement is to help preserve the political miracle that occurred in 1787 in Philadelphia—the creation of a government of laws and not of men.

But there are those, as this history illustrates, who reject the Founders' principles and a Jurisprudence of Original Constitutional Meaning. They favor a judiciary that is governed simply by what it views as politically desirable at a particular time and substitutes its own views and prejudices for the rule of law.

Such an idea dangerously weakens the Constitution and undermines the checks and balances in our political system—safeguards that have protected us against all forms of tyranny since the founding of the Republic. It was John Marshall in *Marbury v. Madison* who pointed out that the Constitution is a limitation on judicial as well as executive and legislative power. And it was Chief Justice Marshall in *McCulloch v. Maryland* who cautioned judges never to forget that it is a Constitution they are expounding. The freedom-based public interest law movement was established to defend the original meaning of constitutional provisions and statutes as the only reliable guide for bringing justice to the people.

As related in Chapter 1, 30 years ago the term "public interest law" was generally used to describe groups of attorneys around the country—mostly liberal in their political views—that had turned from representing individual poor people with their ordinary legal problems to maintaining novel legal actions on behalf of political activists and special-interest social causes. Often these lawsuits sought to nullify public policy decisions made by the citizens of a community or state, who had acted through their elected representatives or by their own majority votes in initiative and referendum elections. These so-called public interest lawyers were usually supported by government funds gained from taxes or by mandatory fees; but there was no equal opportunity for representation of those members of the public who often were the targets of the litigation that ensued: taxpayers, property owners, school children, business entrepreneurs, and law-abiding citizens.

It was to fill this void that the freedom-based public interest law movement was created. Funded by concerned private citizens, philanthropic individuals and foundations, civic groups, and business and professional organizations, dedicated young lawyers took up the cudgels against a vast array of well-financed liberal attorneys.

The pattern had been set some five years earlier, when the National Right to Work Legal Defense Foundation was established to protect the nation's workers from improper labor conduct and union coercion. Now these specialized labor law attorneys were joined by general litigation organizations ready to handle a wide variety of legal needs.

The chapters of this book depict how idealistic and exceptionally skilled lawyers, who have eschewed the blandishments of highly remunerative law firm positions, have made legal history on behalf of the genuine public interest. Their reward has not been massive contingent fees, but the knowledge that they have contributed to individual liberty, limited government, free enterprise, and stronger family life and moral values.

This history, however, is a progress report about a vital ongoing movement, not the final account of a completed work. The challenges continue, the legal issues are more subtle and complex, and the increasingly well-funded opposition has expanded the intensity of its activities.

- Anti-religion forces, ignoring the constitutional prohibition against government interference with religious expression, still try to remove any recognition of God from the public square.
- Attempts to allow parents greater choice in their children's education now face state constitutional provisions concerning public aid to church-sponsored schools that were enacted many decades ago as a result of religious bigotry.
- Land and environmental regulations, as well as the improper use of the power of eminent domain, still constitute a significant threat to private property.
- The Boy Scouts of America, despite a U.S. Supreme Court decision in their favor, still face bigoted and hostile attacks because they—and similar organizations—stand up for traditional moral values as they exercise their First Amendment freedoms.

- Colleges and universities, which should be citadels of free speech and marketplaces for the free expression of ideas, still resort to oppressive regulations and punitive action against views that are not "politically correct" or that are counter to ultra-liberal orthodoxy.

- A recent unfortunate Supreme Court decision has provided a loophole for those who would seek to prolong racial discrimination through the use of preferences and quotas in higher education admission practices. There are still too many in high places in both government and business who refuse to fully implement the constitutional promise that all persons are created equal and that our nation deserves to have a color-blind society.

These are just a few of the challenges that face our country and provide opportunities for the freedom-based public interest law movement. The potential for success depends a great deal on the support these organizations receive from public-spirited donors who seek a nation that continues to follow the Constitution, the principles of the Founders, and the rule of law.

In preparing for this book, leaders of the pro-freedom law movement expressed their views on the course that should be set for the years ahead.

First and foremost is to continue the high quality of lawyering that has characterized the work of the freedom-based public interest groups and has produced the victories of the past three decades.

Second is the expanded filing of *amicus curiae* briefs to counteract the growing tendency of some judges to succumb to pressure from liberal political, legal, and news media sources to rule according to elitist "fashions of the moment" and abdicate their duty to state objectively what the law is as enacted by the people's representatives.

Public interest law firms, in cooperation with related professional and public policy organizations, should teach the skills of lawyering and policymaking, as well as concepts of ethical conduct and true public service. This should be done in the context of our nation's heritage and the principles of law and government under our Constitution. Intern programs, professional lectures and seminars, mentoring programs, and other educational resources should be made available, not only to benefit new and aspiring public interest lawyers, but also to create a reserve corps of lawyers from which freedom-oriented administrations at both the federal and state levels can draw talented and energetic recruits.

To the extent possible, the educational function of public interest law groups should be enhanced by clinic and seminar programs at open-minded law schools. Likewise, opportunities should be provided for law professors to work at public interest firms during summers and sabbatical periods so that they can contribute their academic knowledge and also enhance their own experience through real-world trial and appellate advocacy.

Against great odds and a powerful entrenched legal establishment, the freedom-based public interest law movement has accomplished much, but much remains to be done. At the heart of this enterprise is the Constitution, which represents the will of the people in an enduring political sense. The Constitution does not and should not merely mirror the wishes of each passing majority in the body politic or in the politicized opinions of judges, however distinguished. The foundation of the rule of law is the Constitution, faithfully interpreted as to its true meaning by an independent judiciary that understands and is faithful to its constitutional role.

Historian Russell Kirk suggested four primary characteristics of a good constitution, which bear repeating here and which lie at the heart of the freedom-based public interest law movement:

- *A good constitution should provide for stability and continuity in the governing of a country.*
- *A good constitution should divide political power among different branches of government and should restrain government*

from assuming powers that belong to other social organizations, social classes, or individuals.

- *A good constitution should establish a permanent arrangement by which holders of political authority are representative of the people they govern.*

- *A good constitution should hold accountable the persons who govern a state or a country.*

We in America are fortunate that our nation has just such a constitution: one that is worth preserving and protecting against all enemies, foreign and domestic.

That is the mission of the freedom-based public interest law movement. The following pages provide an exciting narrative of the movement's significant progress over the past 30 years. And they outline how great, and important, is the opportunity for the movement's future success in bringing justice to the people.

CHAPTER 1

The First Thirty Years

Lee Edwards

The freedom-based public interest law movement was born in the early 1970s in reaction to several accelerating trends in America: an activist Supreme Court and federal judiciary, an intrusive regulatory government, continuing legislative activism, and an expanding liberal public interest law coalition. The freedom-based movement's founders were also driven to action because they understood they could not turn for recourse to a Democrat-controlled Congress that strongly supported all of these trends.

At the same time, the founders benefited from a significant political development: the growing strength and influence of a national conservative movement committed to fundamental American ideas such as limited government, the free market, individual freedom and responsibility, and a belief in God—all bounded by the Constitution. From the beginning, then, the freedom-based public interest law movement was dually motivated—by an abiding respect for the original meaning of the Constitution and a determination to oppose the radical agenda of the liberal establishment.

Perhaps the most disturbing development in American law in modern times has been the transformation of the Supreme Court of the United States from judicial arbiter into avid policymaker. In its post–World War II activist phase, the Court has interpreted the Constitution so as to ban prayer in public schools and crèches in public buildings, require that children be bussed miles away from their neighborhoods, declare there is a constitutional right to have an abortion, protect pornography under the rubric of free speech, permit Congress to regulate the nation's non-economic as well as economic activity, and allow the guilty to go unpunished where there are technical flaws in the gathering of evidence.

To justify their decisions and honor their social consciences, justices have either discovered rights in the Constitution that do not exist or simply followed the lead of Chief Justice Charles Evans Hughes, who remarked, "We are under a Constitution, but the Constitution is what the judges say it is." They have disregarded the prudential philosophy of Justice Felix Frankfurter, who said, "As a member of this Court I am not justified in writing my private notions of policy into the Constitution."[1] They have justified the warning of Chief Justice William H. Rehnquist:

> Once we have abandoned the idea that the authority of the courts to declare laws unconstitutional is somehow tied to the language of the Constitution that the people adopted, a judiciary exercising the power of judicial review appears in a quite different light. Judges then are no longer the keepers of the covenant; instead they are a small group of fortunately situated people with a roving commission to second-guess Congress, state legislatures, and state and federal administrative officers concerning what is best for the country.[2]

The scope of the federal courts' political influence has increasingly widened, political scientist James Q. Wilson notes, as more groups and interests have gained access to the courts, as the judges serving on them have developed a more activist stance, and as Congress has passed more laws containing vague or equivocal language, allowing ready bureaucrats to step in and do the interpreting. Whereas in other political arenas such as Congress, the influence of the contending groups usually depends on their size and resources, the impact of plaintiff and defendant before the courts depends chiefly on the effectiveness of their arguments and—a crucial point made by Wilson—on "the attitudes of the judges." The prevailing attitude of an increasing number of judges has been that of the late Justice William J. Brennan Jr., who wrote that "The genius of our Constitution resides not in any static meaning that it had in a world that is dead and gone, but in the adaptability of its great principles to cope with the problems of a developing America."[3]

The courts have also become more powerful as government has come to play a larger and more permanent role in our lives. The founding father of contemporary activist government was Franklin D. Roosevelt, who explained in 1932 that the New Deal was not a political slogan but "a changed *concept* of the duty and responsibility of Government." Government, Roosevelt said flatly, now "has a final responsibility for the well-being of its citizens."[4]

Such a declaration of governmental responsibility was in direct conflict with the ideas embodied in the Declaration of Independence and the Constitution. The Founders of the Republic strove to create a government strong enough to meet the threats to the safety and happiness of the people, yet not so strong as to become a threat to the liberty of the people. Borrowing from Montesquieu, the Founders separated all legislative, executive, and judicial powers and then, in a radical departure from all previous polities, placed ultimate sovereignty in the hands of the people. The sovereign people delegated to the national government only certain enumerated powers, leaving the remaining powers to be exercised by the state governments or the people themselves.

The New Deal radically altered the balance, giving the federal government new, almost unlimited power and responsibility and giving birth to the modern regulatory state. Every succeeding President through Jimmy Carter accepted Roosevelt's redefinition of government's role and acted predictably. By the mid-1970s, there were 2.8 million federal civilian employees disbursing subsidies, transferring monies to state and local governments, and devising and enforcing regulations. Bureaucrats could determine the owner of a television station, the safety features of an automobile, the drugs allowed on the market.

A hundred new federal agencies sprang up to interpret and enforce a thousand new regulations. The Age of Regulatory Government had arrived. The Constitution, legal scholar Roger Pilon of the Cato Institute points out, lists just three federal crimes: treason, piracy, and counterfeiting. Yet today there are more than 3,000 federal crimes and perhaps 300,000 federal regulations that carry criminal sanctions.

One of the more controversial new federal agencies is the Legal Services Corporation, founded in 1974 as a successor to the legal aid program of the Office of Economic Opportunity (OEO). The early 1960s, economics professor Charles K. Rowley of George Mason University writes, produced new ideas regarding aid for the poor, notably that legal services could be part of an overall anti-poverty program. Although there was no reference to legal aid for the poor in the Economic Opportunity Act of 1964, federal money for such services became available in 1965 for the first time.[5] And the policy thrust of the OEO's legal services shifted from the concept of individual client service toward what liberal lawyers saw as law reform for the poor. By 1970, its legal services program employed about 2,200 lawyers and serviced about 500,000 clients, paying special attention to the development of law centers at progressive law schools.

Following a widely circulated 1971 article in the *Yale Law Journal*, the idea of a national legal services corporation spread rapidly until it was at last enacted by Congress and signed into law by President Richard Nixon in 1974. For the next 20 years, until the election in 1994 of a Republican House of Representatives, which began cutting back its budget and restricting its ideological activities, the Legal Services Corporation played a central part in legal changes and class-action suits supporting an expanded federal government, an attendant bureaucracy, and a weakened federalism. By then, the corporation was distributing $400 million annually to more than three hundred private legal aid groups around the country.

An Iron Triangle

The bureaucratic power of agencies like the Legal Services Corporation is significantly strengthened when government agencies and departments form an iron triangle with the congressional committees entrusted with their oversight and with special-interest groups and their legal aid allies. There are, in fact, more politically active special-interest groups in America than in any other country in the world. Many got their start in the 1960s, when young people were strongly influenced by the activism of the civil rights and anti-war movements and when college enrollments more than doubled. The most enduring of these activists is undoubtedly Ralph Nader, who became a national figure in the mid-1960s after General Motors made a clumsy attempt to discredit his background when he was testifying before Congress in favor of an auto safety bill.

With a large out-of-court settlement against GM and the royalties from his best-selling muckraking books, Nader founded Public Citizen and then a variety of other groups that by early 1978 included Congress Watch, Critical Mass (against nuclear energy), Public Citizen Litigation Group, and Health Research Group. Nader also helped start local Public Interest Research Groups (PIRGs), which have become an influential part of the liberal public interest law movement. The first PIRG set the activist pattern for the many that followed. One of its attorneys petitioned the Food and Drug Administration to require disclosures of the phosphate content of laundry detergent. Two attorneys moved to West Virginia to mobilize community opposition to what they claimed were Union Carbide's "inadequate" air pollution controls.[6]

Nader's Public Citizen Litigation Group has initiated dozens of lawsuits on behalf of the public, taking 29 cases in its first two decades to the Supreme Court. They have had a significant impact on many areas of law, including occupational safety and health, lawyers' ethics, and the constitutional separation of powers. One Litigation Group lawsuit—*INS v. Chadha*—resulted in the Supreme Court declaring the "legislative veto" to be unconstitutional. The group became so successful that it started a Supreme Court Assistance Project to help litigators devise winning strategies for their cases before the Court.

The ever-restless Nader also helped establish the Equal Justice Foundation to battle for such legal changes as expanded standing rules and Trial Lawyers for Public Justice, which undertakes tort litigation against government and corporate "wrongdoing." Nader likes to boast that "three good lawyers devoted to the public interest could overthrow the corrupt administration of a major American city."[7] As laudable as many of Nader's populist causes may have been, however, liberal lawyers have used similar techniques to advance elitist goals in such areas as school choice and religious liberty.

The Birth of Legal Aid

The first legal aid organization in America, according to Charles K. Rowley, was established in 1876 by the German Society in New York. It provided assistance in landlord–tenant disputes and family law and helped discourage exploitation of German immigrants by "runners, boardinghouse keepers and a miscellaneous coterie of sharpers."[8] Over time, the New York and Chicago societies were joined by hundreds of similar organizations as well as criminal-defense agencies, all supported by charitable donations from private rather than governmental sources.

But legal assistance for the poor remained uneven and limited to larger cities. At last, the American Bar Association created a Special

Committee on Legal Aid, chaired by Charles Evans Hughes, which recommended the establishment of a National Association of Legal Aid Organizations, later the National Legal Aid and Defender Association. Organizers, says Rowley, worked through local bar associations to establish legal aid societies with varying degrees of success. The American legal aid movement was significantly affected in the late 1940s by the formation of the British Legal Aid and Advice System. The possibility of a similar government-financed program in the United States led state and local bar associations to expand their legal aid work. Over the next decade, the percentage of large cities without legal aid offices sharply declined from 43 percent to 21 percent. By the early 1960s, some 160 organizations provided legal assistance to the poor, with an aggregate budget of just under $4.5 million.

However, a 90-year tradition of private legal aid ended in 1965, Kenneth F. Boehm and Peter T. Flaherty write, when the federal government began making direct grants to legal aid organizations through the Office of Economic Opportunity. Few local aid societies and bar associations could resist accepting the federal funds freely flowing in furtherance of the goals of the highly ideological OEO staff. By the late 1960s, the office was distributing $42 million to 300 organizations, creating a network of law offices and attorneys equal in size to the Department of Justice and all its U.S. attorney offices. In the early 1970s, liberal congressional supporters of legal services moved to insulate the program from political (i.e., conservative Republican) pressure by establishing the Legal Services Corporation, which dispensed even greater sums of federal money (ten times as much by 1994) in much the same partisan manner as the Office of Economic Opportunity.[9]

The Liberal Granddaddy

One organization has led the way in public interest law: the American Civil Liberties Union. From its founding in 1920, the ACLU was a champion of individual rights in the nation—as defender of the First Amendment rights of the Jehovah's Witnesses, initiator of the Scopes Monkey Trial, anti-censorship advocate for the publication of James Joyce's controversial novel *Ulysses*, protestor against the Roosevelt administration's imprisonment of Japanese–Americans during World War II, and protector of the constitutional rights of Nazi leader George Lincoln Rockwell and the Ku Klux Klan.

Under its longtime executive director Roger Baldwin, the ACLU used every available legal instrument, including *amicus curiae* briefs, public protests and publicity, and litigation in the federal and state courts, to stand up for the constitutional rights and liberties of the individual. Although a few state bar and local aid programs provided legal representation to the indigent and controversial, the ACLU led the fight for racial equality, dramatic changes in criminal procedure, and uncompromising protection of free speech. In the headlines and behind the scenes, wrote Pepperdine University professor F. LaGard Smith, the ACLU has been "among America's most influential forces in the defense of individual freedom."[10]

But starting in the 1960s, the ACLU became part—and often the leader—of a public interest law movement so radically nontextual in its interpretation of the Constitution that it considers the teenager's right to have an abortion inviolable but not her ability to pray at her public school graduation, and supports same-sex marriages by gays and lesbians but does not want states to ban child pornography. It is guilty, as LaGard Smith puts it, of extreme moralism (don't discriminate) and extreme relativism (pornography is OK) at the same time. Former federal judge Robert Bork quotes a friend's summing up of the ACLU: "Whether the issue be racial balance in schools, seat belts on autos, or the rules for women's basketball in Iowa, the desires of the people to be affected are given little or no weight by the intellectual class."[11] Once the fearless advocate of the common man, the ACLU has become, all too often, the willing servant of a liberal elite.

The ACLU has been joined by several hundred public interest law firms, the federally funded Legal Services Corporation, Ralph Nader's Public Interest Research Groups, old-line legal groups such as the NAACP Legal Defense and Education Fund, and more recent groups such as People for the American Way. This formidable movement often seems indifferent to—and even opposes—the rights of the traditional family and the unborn, economic liberty and private property, free speech and equal opportunity, federalism and the separation of powers.

A freedom-based reaction to such disregard for the principles of life, liberty, and property as guaranteed under the Constitution was inevitable, and it began, as so much of modern American politics has, in the most populous state of the union: California.

Reagan and Reform

Governor Ronald Reagan had promised welfare reform in his 1970 re-election campaign, and he was determined to deliver on his promise. An initial review of the state's welfare system focused on the costly program Aid to Families with Dependent Children (AFDC). Unless AFDC was curbed, Reagan was warned by advisers, a huge tax increase in the 1972 fiscal year would be necessary. In December 1969, the AFDC rolls listed 1.15 million. A year later, after Reagan's re-election, there were about 1.6 million on the rolls—nearly one out of every 13 Californians.

At the governor's direction, his Chief of Staff, Edwin Meese III, convened a task force to start from scratch and develop a plan for total welfare reform. The task force included Robert B. Carleson, at the time chief deputy director of the state department of public works and later U.S. commissioner of welfare in the Reagan administration; Ned Hutchinson, the governor's appointments secretary and chairman of the task force; Jerry Fielder, director of the state department of agriculture; John Mayfield, assistant director of the state department of conservation; and Reagan himself. Ronald A. Zumbrun, a senior attorney, and John A.

Svahn, an administrative analyst, both with the state department of public works, were called upon for help. Top staff, including Secretary James M. Hall of the state business and transportation agency, were then assigned to develop the administrative, regulatory, and statutory provisions of what became the California Welfare Reform Act.

The act, Reagan biographer Lou Cannon says, was "a seminal achievement" of Reagan's governorship.[12] Eighty-three percent of the honest welfare recipients had their grants increased, while the welfare rolls started to decline immediately. Within three years, the welfare caseload dropped by more than 250,000, and other states, including New York under liberal Governor Nelson Rockefeller, began to enact variations of Reagan's welfare reform. But California's entrenched welfare establishment fought the changes every inch of the way.

The attacks were led by welfare rights organizations, legal aid societies, social worker unions, members of the California Legislature, and many public interest law firms. It became clear to those supporting welfare reform, says Ronald A. Zumbrun in Chapter 2, that "a serious imbalance" existed in the public interest law field. No one was litigating in support of the free enterprise system, private property rights, and a careful weighing of economic, social, *and* environmental concerns. The one exception was the National Right to Work Legal Defense Foundation, which since 1968 had been defending employees' rights against forced unionism (see Chapter 8, "Protecting Workers' Rights," by David Kendrick).

In the middle of 1972, members of Reagan's welfare reform legal team began meeting with other administration officials about the need for a new kind of nonprofit public interest law firm. At the same time, business leader John Simon Fluor was discussing his frustrations over delays of the Alaska pipeline project and offshore drilling in the Gulf of Mexico—delays resulting from lawsuits filed by environmental groups—with California attorney William French Smith, who would later become U.S. attorney general.

In January 1973, a group of Californians, including a prominent attorney and a civil leader from each of the state's six regions, met in San Francisco to discuss the formation of a freedom-based public interest law firm. Ronald Zumbrun was asked to develop a formal proposal, which was adopted in early February. The new organization was named the Pacific Legal Foundation (PLF) and was incorporated a month later. John Simon Fluor was elected chairman of the board and immediately started raising the necessary seed money. "His stature and vision," says Zumbrun, "were a key to PLF's early success." The importance of Governor Reagan's determination to reform welfare can be seen in the fact that 11 of the first individuals to join the foundation's staff had been part of the welfare reform team. Zumbrun subsequently was elevated to president and CEO of the foundation; Roy A. Green was named executive vice president. At last there was a free enterprise answer, albeit modest, to the formidable resources of the old-line liberal legal groups.

When the Pacific Legal Foundation achieved success in California against radical environmental groups, the question was asked: Why not replicate it in other states? Accordingly, the National Legal Center for the Public Interest was founded in 1975 and set out to create a network of public interest law organizations patterned after the Pacific Legal Foundation. Leonard Theberge was the center's first president and in three years created a number of foundations around the country. Among them were the Mountain States Legal Foundation; the Southeastern Legal Foundation; what is now the Atlantic Legal Foundation; and the Gulf and Great Plains Legal Foundation, which became the Landmark Legal Foundation.

Having accomplished the National Legal Center's mission, the board of directors had a choice: Close down the organization or develop a new mission. The board decided there was critical work to be done in the non-litigation field. It moved to Washington, D.C., and selected businessman Ernest B. Hueter as president, a position he has held for almost 24 years. The center fosters knowledge of the law and the administration of justice in a society committed to individual rights, free enterprise, private property, limited government, a balanced use of private and public resources, and a fair and efficient judiciary. It has become one of the best-known non-litigating organizations in the freedom-based public interest law movement through such programs as the annual Gauer Distinguished Lecture in Law and Public Policy and "A Day With Justice," featuring briefings by top officials of the Justice Department for corporate general counsel and business attorneys. But all that was far in the future in the mid-1970s.

The organizational and financial imbalance between the freedom-based and the liberal public interest law movements continued for the rest of the 1970s and into the 1980s. As late as 1988, conservative legal groups had a total of fewer than 50 litigators and combined budgets of less than $11 million, while their philosophical opponents boasted hundreds of lawyers and federal and state funding in the hundreds of millions of dollars. The California Legislature alone provided over $15.5 million in public interest law funding in 1988. However, as Zumbrun notes in Chapter 2, the number of conservative public interest lawyers in 1989 was the same as that of liberal lawyers in 1969, just before their rapid expansion in the 1970s (much of it financed by the Legal Services Corporation).

All public interest law firms specialize in precedent-setting legal action, do not charge for their services, and represent interests that would otherwise not appear before the courts. But freedom-based public interest law firms, Zumbrun points out, face greater challenges than their liberal counterparts. They usually litigate against heavily staffed and funded government agencies as well as radical legal organizations. They are concerned almost exclusively with critical issues that are often decided by the highest courts. They confront a judicial activism—and liberal mass media—strongly opposed to their freedom-based philosophy. Although the pro-freedom public interest law movement initially encountered serious programmatic and fund-raising difficulties, it never abandoned either its resolute defense of the Constitution as written or its basic belief in the American legal system.

Starting in late 1986, the movement began to make a difference in important areas like private property rights. First, the U.S. Supreme Court took jurisdiction in a number of individual rights cases, particularly in the fields of government regulation and land use. Second, three California Supreme Court justices were not re-elected because the public, by a two to one margin, perceived them as judicial lawmakers rather than interpreters. "The lesson to be learned from the California experience," Zumbrun writes, "is that the public will not tolerate judicial activism."

In 1987, the U.S. Supreme Court accepted the arguments of the Pacific Legal Foundation and ruled in *Nollan v. California Coastal Commission* that the commission could not require the plaintiffs to dedicate one-third of their property to the state as a condition of receiving a permit to rebuild their home. The Court called the practice "an out-and-out plan of extortion." *Nollan* is widely accepted as the most important land use case in at least 65 years and has led to a series of victories and precedents in the field.

Among the organizations that have built on *Nollan* is the Southeastern Legal Foundation, which filed suit in Virginia state court in 1998 (*Dail v. York County*) to test local regulation of the forestry industry and whether such regulation constituted a "taking" of reasonable use and enjoyment of private property.

The plaintiff, an elderly widow relying on income from harvesting timber on a forest parcel she had inherited, challenged a county ordinance that set stringent standards for forestry, including submission of an extensive forest management plan for approval by the local zoning board. The widow relied on a new state law that provided that "silvacultural activity ... shall not be prohibited or unreasonably limited by a local government's use of its police, planning and zoning powers." (Va. Code ~ 10.1-1126.1) Virginia law further required that local ordinances pertaining to forestry "shall not be in conflict with the purposes of promoting the growth, continuation and beneficial use of ... privately owned forest resources" advanced by the state law. (Va. Code ~ 10.1-1126.1) Although the plaintiff won on the issue of setbacks and buffers, she lost on the issue of state law trumping the more restrictive local ordinance. The court interpreted the local ordinance as an extension of the state law. In succeeding years, however, the ordinance has been modified to reflect state law. Such are the conflicts and complexities of property rights litigation when competing governmental entities—federal, state, and local—attempt to regulate the use and enjoyment of private property.

Government also can violate constitutional limitations on land use exactions, another increasingly familiar issue at the state and local levels. The Southeastern Legal Foundation filed suit against the city of Atlanta, challenging the implementation of its development impact fee program. (*Greater Atlanta Home Builders Association v. City of Atlanta*) Following *Nollan* and *Dolan v. City of Tigard*, Georgia outlawed land use exactions that did not have the required nexus to projects seeking permits for new development.

Local governments must now use engineering and planning experts to determine the areas containing public facilities such as roads, parks, and public safety facilities. They must also provide the infrastructure needed for high-growth areas. And they must set a level of service that the facilities must continue to furnish as the area grows. But in contradiction of the constraints imposed by the Takings Clause of the Constitution and the Georgia statute, Atlanta has used millions of dollars in fees it has collected from developers to fund improvements in the infrastructure of a different part of the city—in an attempt to encourage development. At stake, argues the Southeastern Legal Foundation, is a constitutional issue regarding the "property rights" attached to special fees paid by individuals for specific government services. *Greater Atlanta Home Builders Association* is one of the first major federal court cases on this issue and will produce important case law precedent.

School Choice

The Supreme Court's ruling in *Zelman v. Simmons-Harris* in 2002 was not only a landmark decision in school choice, but also, Clint Bolick writes in Chapter 3, "a milestone in the evolution, maturation, and effectiveness of the pro-freedom public interest law movement."

In the fall of 1990, Landmark Legal Foundation initiated litigation to force Wisconsin public education officials to implement the Milwaukee Parental Choice Program. Representing the program's legislative sponsor, Wisconsin State Representative Polly Williams, and low-income children eligible to participate in the program, Landmark set in motion the 12-year journey to the *Zelman* ruling. Joined by the Institute for Justice and an outstanding team of private attorneys led by Kenneth Starr, Landmark tenaciously fought their way to victory in a series of cases involving the Milwaukee program. What began as a small pilot program grew over time—and with successive courtroom victories—into the nation's first and most successful school choice program affording low-income children access to religious and nonreligious private schools.

Freedom-based litigators learned important lessons in their long march. One, a largely untapped opportunity exists for pro-freedom public interest groups to defend reform legislation in the state courts. Two, it is important not to leave the legal defense of such programs to state attorneys general who, however well meaning, are subject to "political aspirations and pressures." Three, the best way to preserve a program is to invest legal resources in its creation to make it as legally defensible as possible.

In anticipation of an appearance before the U.S. Supreme Court, the pro-freedom attorneys met with Establishment Clause scholars who counseled them to emphasize that the case was about education, not religion. The attorneys had to make it clear, Bolick writes, that the central issue was "really about educational opportunities for children who desperately needed them," a theme that "permeated both our legal tactics and rhetoric."

When they reached the Supreme Court, the pro-freedom attorneys used as a "legal hook" the Establishment Clause's "primary effect" test, which all parties agreed governed the case, and translated it into a real world standard. They talked about the crisis of inner-city education, the emergency in the Cleveland public schools, and the benefits of school choice for minority children. They often invoked *Brown v. Board of Education*, triggering "a hysterical response" from the NAACP Legal Defense and Education Fund that served to highlight the pro-freedom argument. A key tactic, Bolick says, was to ensure that every legal contributor and every page of every brief "made a distinctive point" or reinforced critical points in a different but persuasive way.

Liberal as well as conservative academics and attorneys were folded into the legal team. "Our view," Bolick explains, "was the broader [in philosophy and background] the team, the more likely we could communicate effectively with each member of the Court." An "ecumenical approach" to litigation, he feels, is essential "to the public interest legal enterprise." Also important is the court of public opinion: On the day of the Supreme Court argument, there was a massive rally of parents and children from across the country in front of the Court building. As the Left recognized decades ago, Bolick concludes, "law is a powerful tool for social change. Those of us who are lucky enough to be pro-freedom litigators have opportunities that are bound only by our passion and imagination."

Another battle for school choice has been waged by the Atlantic Legal Foundation, which is counseling or representing charter schools in New York and New Jersey through its Parental Choice in Education program. The foundation has also established a lawyers' clearinghouse, matching the needs of charter schools—whether for counseling in corporate or regulatory matters or in litigation—with attorneys willing to help *pro bono*.

The Battle for Religious Liberty

Although it had heard oral arguments just two months earlier, the Supreme Court ruled in December 1981 in *Widmar v. Vincent* that the Constitution protected the freedom of speech rights of students at the University of Missouri-Kansas City to meet on campus for a weekly evangelical worship service. By 8 to 1, the court rejected the university's argument that the Constitution's Establishment Clause required the school to ban such meetings. Attorneys James Smart and Michael Whitehead, says Alan E. Sears in Chapter 4, were among the first public interest lawyers fighting in the courts for religious liberty as well as the sanctity of life and traditional marriage.

An earlier legal champion of religious liberty was William Bentley Ball, who urged the Supreme Court throughout the 1970s to stop its extreme interpretations of the Establishment Clause in cases like *Lemon v. Kurtzman*. Ball won a major victory in *Wisconsin v. Yoder* when the court upheld the right of an Amish family to opt out of a Wisconsin law requiring them to send their children to public schools on the grounds that it would conflict with their religious beliefs. Ball remained active before the Supreme Court into the 1980s and 1990s, gaining a significant win in *Zobrest v. Catalina Foothills School District*, a 1993 case that helped to pave the way for many of the later favorable school choice decisions.

Several religious liberty litigation groups sprang up following the *Widmar* victory, including the Rutherford Institute under John Whitehead (no relation to Michael Whitehead). Michael Farris moved from Washington State to Washington, D.C., to start two legal operations: the litigation arm of Beverly LaHaye's Concerned Women for America and the Home School Legal Defense Association. Both groups won telling legal victories in the following years, including a unanimous Supreme Court decision in *Witters v. Washington Department of Services for the Blind*. Writing for the majority, Justice Thurgood Marshall stated that the Establishment Clause did not justify a Washington state law singling out theology as the only major for which blind people could not study if they received funding from an education fund for disabled persons.

It is important to note, says Sears, that these groups "tackled more than just religious liberty issues." They viewed their purpose as the preservation of a "traditional American legal worldview, one rooted in Judeo–Christian principles." They opposed, for example, *Roe v. Wade*'s alleged right to abortion and the growing threat to constitutional rights posed by homosexual activists. A major success of the freedom-based religious liberty organizations was the effort to establish the right of parents to home school their children. All of this heightened activity led to the emergence of expert constitutional litigators like Jay Sekulow, who successfully defended the right of students to establish religious clubs in public schools in *Board of Education v. Mergens*. In 2001, the Supreme Court again ruled in favor of equal access for public school students in *Good News Club v. Milford Central School*.

The effectiveness of religious liberty groups increased exponentially in 1993 when more than 30 religious leaders, including Dr. Bill Bright of Campus Crusade for Christ, Dr. James Dobson of Focus on the Family, Dr. D. James Kennedy of Coral Ridge Ministries, and Larry Burkett of Crown Financial Ministries, endorsed the formation of the Alliance Defense Fund. Alan Sears was named the first president and CEO of the Alliance Defense Fund, positions he has held ever since.

The ADF's mission, explains Sears, is to "provide the training, coordination, and funding for all of the religious liberty groups so that no case will be lost because of lack of resources or experience." Within a year of opening its doors, the fund helped win two consequential Supreme Court cases: the Boston St. Patrick's Day parade case (*Hurley v. Irish-American Gay, Lesbian and Bisexual Group of Boston*) and *Rosenberger v. Rector*, which involved a discriminatory funding system at the University of Virginia that excluded only student Christian publications.

The importance of the Alliance Defense Fund's existence, argues Sears, can be seen when one considers the nearly solitary labor of attorney James Smart in *Widmar* more than 20 years ago. Smart had no funding except for a few hundred dollars donated by the students at the University of Missouri. He had no access to experienced Supreme Court advocates to help him prepare his oral arguments before the Court. He could not afford to coordinate *amicus* briefs to support him; and in fact there were only a few groups capable of preparing briefs. Although James Smart won, mainly due to his heroic personal efforts, the Alliance Defense Fund—which has provided millions of dollars to support litigation—exists "to make sure that important cases do not have to labor under so many impediments to victory."

Meanwhile, beginning in 1996, Mountain States Legal Foundation litigated to prevent the closure of federal (public) land to congressionally mandated economic and recreation activity because the land was purportedly "sacred" to some American Indians. Although the Supreme Court had barred such closures in 1988, under the Clinton administration federal land managers found that protecting the demands of land-based religion worshipers was as useful as protecting the needs of endangered species and "wetlands" in order to place more lands off-limits to Westerners. The foundation's first litigation involved the closure of Devils Tower in Wyoming to non-Indian climbers, but soon included the closure of one million acres of the Lewis and Clark National Forest in Montana to oil and gas exploration; the closure of 50,000 acres of the Bighorn National Forest in Wyoming to timber harvesting; and the bar against visitors approaching Rainbow Bridge in Utah, the world's largest natural arch, because some American Indians regard the arch as God incarnate.

Economic Liberty

One of the most shocking impediments to freedom in our country is the relegation of economic liberty to second-class status under the Constitution. This denial of economic liberty, William H. Mellor points out in Chapter 5, is due to two Supreme Court decisions—the *Slaughter-House Cases* of 1872 and *United States v. Carolene Products* in 1938—that have allowed economic regulation at the federal, state, and local levels to prevail virtually unchecked ever since.

Economic regulation dramatically increased in the 1960s and 1970s through the legal advocacy of such new liberal groups as the Natural Resources Defense Council, Public Citizen, and the Legal Services Corporation and old-line organizations like the ACLU and the Sierra Club, all of which urged a greater governmental role in economic and property matters. So effective were their efforts that attorney Lewis Powell (a future Supreme Court justice) wrote an article for the U.S. Chamber of Commerce in which he stated, "The judiciary may be the most important instrument of social, economic, and political change."

As bleak as the current state of affairs regarding economic liberty is, Mellor suggests there are trends that offer hope for eventually overturning the *Slaughter-House Cases* and restoring "constitutional vitality to the Privileges or Immunities Clause." The first is the maturing of the freedom-based public interest law movement, putting advocates of economic liberty in courtrooms across America. Groups such as the Institute for Justice, the Pacific Legal Foundation, the Landmark Legal Foundation, the New England Legal Foundation, the Atlantic Legal Foundation, and the Mountain States Legal Foundation have all pursued cutting-edge litigation seeking to roll back the excesses of the *Carolene Products* decision.

The second is the growing body of scholarship that challenges the moral and legal underpinnings of the *Slaughter-House Cases*. The Supreme Court has suggested the possibility of revisiting the Privileges or Immunities Clause and also has indicated a willingness to recognize some "outer boundaries" on heretofore unchecked government authority, as in *Lucas v. South Carolina Coastal Council*. At the same time, says Mellor, there is "a mounting consensus" that recognizes the failure of the welfare state to truly help the disadvantaged, particularly in the inner city, opening up the opportunity for more inner-city enterprise freed of government restraints and regulations.

To decide what should replace the philosophy of the *Slaughter-House Cases*, Mellor writes, there is no better place to start than the dissents of justices Bradley, Field, and Swayne. Reaching back to Adam Smith and the founding of the Republic, Justice Bradley recognized the right "of every American citizen to adopt and follow lawful industrial pursuit—not injurious to the community—as he may see fit without unreasonable regulation or molestation."

And then there is the environment. Since the country's founding, Congress had regarded the federal government's vast landholdings—it owns one-third of the nation's land, mostly in the West—as primarily a source of economic activity for rural communities that had grown up with federal government assistance in the midst of these lands. In some Western counties, as much as 60, 70, 80, and even 90 percent of the land is federally owned. Therefore, economic activity requires the use of adjacent federal lands. A host of federal statutes not only permitted such activity, but also encouraged it.

But with the dawn of the environmental movement in 1970, well-funded groups demanded that Congress pass new laws and that federal judges reinterpret old laws to prevent economic and recreational activity on federal lands. Industries such as oil and gas exploration and development, mining, and forestry that had provided high-paying jobs were soon under economic siege. Descendants of those who had settled the West—ranchers and farmers—were besieged.

Mountain States Legal Foundation, founded in 1977 by Colorado businessman Joseph Coors, was created to defend the Western men, women, and communities that were no match for the massive federal bureaucracy, with its thousands of lawyers, and the environmental organizations and their litigation and public relations juggernaut. Proving that one organization can make a difference, it defended President Reagan's Western economic initiative, resulting in two key rulings by the Supreme Court that limit the ability of environmental groups to get standing to sue.

The foundation not only has litigated to set legal precedent, but also has worked to change public attitudes about environmental policy. It defended, for example, sheepherder John Shuler, who was prosecuted by the U.S. Fish and Wildlife Service for killing a grizzly bear in self-defense. The foundation won the eight-year battle and turned Shuler, with the help of *Reader's Digest*, Rush Limbaugh, and others into a symbol for what is wrong with the Endangered Species Act. Over the years, other groups such as the Pacific Legal Foundation, Landmark Legal Foundation, and Washington Legal Foundation have joined the environmental battle.

Equality Under the Law

While there is a broad national consensus that discrimination based on race, ethnicity, and sex is wrong, many government entities, including courts, have concluded that discrimination against whites, men, and so-called over-represented minority groups is not only permissible but essential. As a result, affirmative action is widespread, and quotas and other preferential practices prevail throughout the country. Such politically correct discrimination, Roger Clegg says in Chapter 6, would be far more widespread were it not for the freedom-based public interest legal movement.

In landmark case after case—such as *Adarand Constructors, Inc. v. Peña, Gratz v. Bollinger, Hopwood v. Texas, Shaw v. Reno*, and *Podberesky v. Kirwan*—litigating groups like the Mountain States Legal Foundation, Pacific Legal Foundation, Center for Individual Rights, Landmark Legal Foundation, Institute for Justice, Southeastern Legal Foundation, Washington Legal Foundation, and Individual Rights Foundation have played critical and difficult roles.

Mountain States Legal Foundation was part of the "Sagebrush Rebellion," in which Westerners objected to the restrictions placed on their ability to engage in economic and recreational activity on federal lands. It initially focused on natural resources and environmental laws but soon began working to help non-minority contractors who were denied jobs due to their race.

In August 1990, the foundation filed a complaint for Adarand Constructors, Inc., in federal district court, setting in motion a long journey through the federal system that included three appearances before the Supreme Court. The most significant occurred in January 1995 when William Perry Pendley, the foundation's president and chief legal officer, argued brilliantly for Adarand. Five months later, the Court issued its ruling in favor of Adarand, holding that there was no difference between what the Constitution required of state and local governments, as set forth in *City of Richmond v. J.A. Croson, Co.*, and what it required of the federal government. "It is difficult," says Clegg, "to overstate the importance of the Supreme Court's 1995 *Adarand* ruling." *Time* called it "a legal earthquake, throwing into doubt most of the government's affirmative action programs."[13]

Those who challenge affirmative action, Clegg writes, risk ostracism. Politicians beholden to special interests refuse to question the programs and often try to expand them. Funds to mount a challenge are hard to find. Members of the legal establishment—including academics, corporate attorneys, and judges—are unsympathetic or hostile. Nevertheless, freedom-based legal groups have stepped into the breach to defend the principles of equal protection that are enshrined in law, cherished by most Americans, and "essential for the survival of our increasingly multiracial, multiethnic nation."

The Pacific Legal Foundation's decades-long battle against government-sponsored race and sex discrimination was greatly aided in November 1996 with the passage of California's Proposition 209, which amended the state constitution to make it illegal for the government to "discriminate against, or grant preferential treatment to, any individual or group on the basis of race, sex, color, ethnicity, or national origin" in the areas of public employment, education, or contracting. The day after Proposition 209 passed, notes Clegg, a federal lawsuit was filed challenging the prohibition of racial discrimination on the ground that "it discriminated on the basis of race [*sic*]." With the help of the Pacific Legal Foundation and briefs filed by other freedom-based legal organizations, the Ninth Circuit Court of Appeals upheld Proposition 209 in *Coalition for Economic Equity v. Wilson*.

In the most important-ever challenge to race-based admissions in higher education, the Center for Individual Rights filed lawsuits in 1997 against the University of Michigan Law School and undergraduate College of Literature, Science, and the Arts. The goal of *Grutter v. Bollinger* and *Gratz v. Bollinger* was to eliminate—at the University of Michigan and nationally—the use of race-based admission systems that employed different, lower admissions standards for minority applicants in order to boost minority enrollment.

In June 2003, after victories and defeats in the lower courts, the Supreme Court issued a split decision, striking down the university's

20-point bonus for college applicants while upholding race-based admission policies at the law school. In the "disappointing law school decision," Clegg states, the Court found campus diversity compelling enough to justify some consideration of race, but did set limits of time and scope to racial admissions preferences.

The Washington Legal Foundation, based in the District of Columbia, has filed *amicus* briefs in several dozen important civil rights cases over the years and played a leading role in *Podberesky v. Kirwan*, which it won before the Fourth Circuit Court of Appeals. The combination of *Podberesky* and *Hopwood v. Texas* (a Center for Individual Rights case) effectively ended efforts by the higher education establishment to justify racial preferences as necessary to overcome past discrimination.

The Individual Rights Foundation is the legal arm of the Center for the Study of Popular Culture, located in Los Angeles. IRF general counsel Manny Klausner has been engaged in constitutional law, election law, and business litigation for four decades. He helped draft Proposition 209 and served as vice chairman—with Ward Connerly as chairman—of the "Yes on 209" campaign. In September 2000, the foundation took up race-based preferences in the Los Angeles Fire Department when it represented David Alexander, a paramedic denied a job because of a 1974 residency requirement that was specifically intended to limit the number of whites in the applicant pool. Los Angeles settled Alexander's case in July 2001 and hired him as a firefighter. But the Individual Rights Foundation was not satisfied. In April 2003, with Alexander and another white firefighter applicant as their clients, the foundation successfully challenged Los Angeles' affirmative action program, which was subsequently declared unconstitutional by Los Angeles Superior Court Judge Helen Bendix.

Although the Center for Equal Opportunity, headed by Linda Chavez, is not a public interest litigation organization, it has courageously fought racial and ethnic preferences since its 1995 founding. Along with the American Civil Rights Institute, chaired by Ward Connerly, the Center for Equal Opportunity has sponsored ballot initiatives across the country to end the use of racial and ethnic preferences and classifications by government. It has also challenged racially exclusive programs at about 100 universities. The majority of schools contacted, including Princeton, the University of Virginia, and the University of Texas, have responded positively.

The center has also drafted model state legislation and freedom of information requests that would require schools to reveal whether and how race is weighed in admissions. Other litigation organizations in the freedom-based public interest law movement, Clegg states, have played their part in the fight against preferences based on race, ethnicity, and sex. There is, for example, the Atlantic Legal Foundation, which forced the state of New Jersey to abandon its use of public contracting preferences in *GEOD Corporation v. New Jersey.*

Another staunch defender of the principle of equality under the law is the Southeastern Legal Foundation, which filed suit in 1998 against President Bill Clinton, the Department of Commerce, and the Census Bureau, challenging the government's plan to use statistical sampling in the 2000 census. The plan proposed that 90 percent of the population be counted by the Census Bureau while the remaining 10 percent—some 27 million Americans—would be statistically projected as to who they are and where they live. The foundation argued that sampling violates the Constitution's mandate that the census be conducted as an "actual Enumeration" performed by "counting the whole number of persons in each state." (U.S. Constitution, Article 1, Section 2)

The Enumeration Clause is the linchpin of the Constitution's approach to the apportionment of political power. Unique among nations, the United States delegates representation in Congress according to the number of persons identified in the decennial census. The Census Act also strictly limits the use of statistical sampling.

After prevailing on expedited review by a three-judge panel in the Fourth Circuit, the Southeastern Legal Foundation proceeded to the Supreme Court where it argued that the sampling would subject the entire census to possible statistical error and lead to a lack of credibility in the political process because sampled numbers were capable of manipulation. In effect, argued the foundation, the sampled census would add "virtual people" invented by the Census Bureau to account for undercounted groups. (*Clinton v. Glavin*) A "virtual" headcount would have resulted in a massive reapportionment of legislatures at both the federal and state levels.

In early 1999, in an unusually speedy decision, the Supreme Court ruled that the use of statistical sampling for purposes of apportionment violated the Census Act. The Court thereby preserved the intention of the Framers that political power should be apportioned to the people based on an actual enumeration of the population, and it protected the integrity of the census process from statistical manipulation.

The liberal opposition is well entrenched and well financed, Clegg concedes, but the Pacific Legal Foundation, the Washington Legal Foundation, the Center for Individual Rights, and other groups are developing case law against discrimination and preferences that, while not perfect and still evolving, protects the rights of millions of Americans.

Freedom of Speech

On matters of free speech, writes Thor L. Halvorssen in Chapter 7, new legal organizations such as the American Civil Rights Union, headed by Robert Carleson, and the American Center for Law and Justice, whose general counsel is Jay Sekulow, seek cooperation across the political spectrum. Other freedom-based public interest groups such as the Atlantic Legal Foundation and the Mountain States Legal Foundation are organized geographically, and still others, such as the Becket Fund for Religious Liberty and Americans United for Life (one of the earliest), confine themselves to specific issues like the right to life. Most freedom of speech cases have occurred in the field of education.

In the area of political protest, writes Halvorssen, the movement has contributed in cases involving the freedom of speech rights of pro-life protesters and political extremists. In school voucher cases, the movement's attorneys have defended freedom of association and freedom of speech in upholding the right of parents to choose a religious school when "they consider it best for their children's educational needs." The movement has produced a string of victories for voluntary association in almost every part of American life, from primary schools and universities to civic organizations and clubs such as the Boy Scouts. In electoral politics, the freedom-based public interest law movement is engaged in challenging the restrictions on freedom of speech that are masked under the term "campaign finance reform."

Movement attorneys, argues Halvorssen, have brought about "extraordinary gains" in preventing viewpoint discrimination against college student groups. *Rosenberger v. Rector* made its way in 1995 to the Supreme Court where Michael W. McConnell and Michael P. McDonald of the Center for Individual Rights argued for the plaintiff. *Amicus* briefs were filed by such groups as the American Center for Law and Justice, the Christian Legal Society, and the Intercollegiate Studies Institute, a conservative educational group that, among other activities, supports alternative student publications. On the other side, the ACLU wrote a brief arguing against the funding of religion on campus.

The Supreme Court ruled that not funding *Wide Awake* (an evangelical Christian student publication edited by Ron Rosenberger) would amount to unconstitutional "viewpoint discrimination." "Vital First Amendment speech principles are at stake here," the Court said. "The first danger to liberty lies in granting the state the power to examine publications to determine whether or not they are based on some ultimate idea and if so for the state to classify them." Writing for the majority, Justice Anthony Kennedy said without equivocation, "There is no Establishment Clause violation in the university's honoring its duties under the Free Speech Clause." The Court's decision, says Halvorssen, meant that universities "could no longer deny funds to students simply because they held religious or controversial points of view."

As campuses became political hotbeds in the 1960s and 1970s, many left-wing student leaders used student fees to finance their activities. Ralph Nader's Public Interest Research Groups collected, it is estimated, millions of dollars from such fees to advance a political agenda focused on consumer issues and the environment. Campus organizations used student fees to promote abortion rights, feminism, and gay and lesbian rights. Some students protested and brought legal action that resulted in at least one case before the Supreme Court.

In *Board of Regents of the University of Wisconsin System v. Southworth*, Jordan Lorence argued for the First Amendment rights of Scott Southworth, who objected to underwriting the activities of radical left groups, such as the International Socialist Organization and the UW Greens, whose viewpoints he abhorred. Central to the First Amendment was Southworth's right *not* to speak. *Amicus* briefs were filed by the Atlantic Legal Foundation, which had previously litigated an important PIRG case in New York; the Pacific Legal Foundation; and the National Legal Foundation. Opposing briefs were submitted by the ACLU, People for the American Way, and the National Education Association.

The Supreme Court agreed that the fees affected Southworth's First Amendment rights and that he had a right not to fund groups he disagreed with if the university distributed the fees in a "viewpoint discriminatory" manner. The Court, however, justified the university's student fee system on the condition that the school funded programs that were "viewpoint neutral." Justice Kennedy wrote that a university "may not prefer some viewpoints to others." The *Southworth* decision reverberated throughout the American academy. One result has been the founding of Collegians for a Constructive Tomorrow to counterbalance what it claims is the PIRGs' radical environmental agenda. Relying on *Southworth*, the collegians have obtained matching funds on several campuses where the PIRGs receive student fee monies.

Perhaps the most important decision protecting voluntary association and freedom of speech came in 2000 with *Boy Scouts of America v. Dale*. Overturning the New Jersey Supreme Court's decision that the Scouts had violated the state's anti-discrimination law when they dismissed a gay Scout leader, the U.S. Supreme Court ruled that forcing the Boy Scouts to accept gays in leadership positions would violate the group's rights to freedom of association and free speech. "The *Dale* decision," writes Halvorssen, "is a new bulwark for pluralism and the safeguarding of diverse viewpoints." The case drew widespread *amicus* support from the Becket Fund for Religious Liberty, the American Center for Law and Justice, the American Civil Rights Union, the Center for Individual Rights, the Southeastern Legal Foundation, the Claremont Institute Center for Constitutional Jurisprudence, and others.

The continuing battle against speech codes, now enforced on hundreds of college campuses, received an important assist in 2003 when the Foundation for Individual Rights in Education coordinated litigation against three codes in U.S. District Courts in *Bair v. Shippensburg University*, *Stevens v. Citrus College*, and *Roberts v. Haragan*. Already, a preliminary injunction has been issued in the *Shippensburg* case, and the *Citrus College* case has been settled to the plaintiff's advantage. Texas Tech has responded to the *Roberts* suit (being handled by the Liberty Legal Institute and the Alliance Defense Fund) by altering policies on its Orwellian "free speech zones."

According to Halvorssen, hundreds of students are persecuted each year for holding views that are "offensive." Many fatalistically accept their situation and submit to university censorship. Others, lacking a legal basis for a claim, are underserved by friends of liberty. But in the past several years, new and existing organizations have begun to vigorously defend free speech on campus and are taking the battle into the courts. Such activities, says Halvorssen, are beginning to shift public opinion as "more and more people understand the importance of addressing universities' illiberal policies." Columnist John Leo of *U.S. News & World Report* argues that the Foundation for Individual Rights in Education, the Center for Individual Rights, and similar pro-freedom legal groups have forced many censorship-minded administrators "into a defensive crouch."

Sound Science in the Law

Since 1993, the Atlantic Legal Foundation has led the legal way in promoting the use of sound science in the adjudicatory and regulatory process. It has represented prominent scientists and scholars, including more that a dozen Nobel laureates, in three Supreme Court decisions that have established the criteria for the admissibility of expert evidence in federal court cases: *Daubert v. Merrell Dow Pharmaceuticals, Inc.* (1993), *General Electric Co. v. Joiner* (1997), and *Kumho Tire Co. v. Carmichael* (1999). ALF's briefs were cited with approval in *Daubert* and *Kumho Tire*. They were also cited as decisive or helpful by the California Supreme Court in a case involving injuries claimed to have been caused by electromagnetic fields and by the Ninth Circuit Court of Appeals in a case in which alleged exposure to a minuscule amount of radioactive material was claimed to have caused the plaintiff's cancer.

The ALF notes that the plaintiff's bar has begun to bring a large number of toxic tort lawsuits involving claims of sickness and property damage allegedly caused by the indoor presence of

mold. The potential exposure of a broad class of defendants—
building owners; mortgage lenders; property and casualty insurance companies; construction companies; producers of building
supplies such as framing, lumber, and roofing materials—is enormous, possibly even greater than that of the lawsuits involving
asbestos. Already insurance companies are declining to issue policies in Texas, where there has been a multi-million dollar judg-
ment against a property insurance company for failing to
promptly correct mold damage. Real estate in Texas has been
seriously affected, making it difficult and in some cases impossible for potential home buyers to obtain mortgage financing.

A critical issue is the admissibility of expert testimony linking
the presence of mold with the alleged injury. Atlantic Legal Foundation's mold initiative focuses on the application of sound science to
the law. Its Web site displays articles discussing the application of
the Supreme Court's decision in *Daubert* and the D.C. Circuit
Court's decision in *Frye v. United States*, abstracts of scientific articles, and citations to relevant federal and state decisions. It offers
the highlights of a two-day conference co-sponsored by the Department of Pharmacology at Georgetown University and the International Center for Toxicology and Medicine. It also identifies
relevant Web sites including recent congressional testimony.

Workers' Rights

The right to voluntarily join a labor union, as well as the right
not to be forced to join a union or pay dues against one's will,
should be a fundamental right of the American worker. Public
interest legal groups began fighting for this right, recounts David
Kendrick in Chapter 8, with the 1968 formation of the National
Right to Work Legal Defense Foundation under the leadership of
Reed Larson. Larson saw how liberal legal aid groups like the
NAACP Legal Defense and Education Fund and the ACLU had
shaped public policy through the years and determined to follow
their example. The resulting legal aid foundation has defended

individual workers against compulsory unionism ever since. At the heart of their work is the constitutional principle, expressed by Thomas Jefferson, that "to compel a man to furnish contributions of money for the propagation of opinions which he disbelieves is sinful and tyrannical."

The Supreme Court accepted this argument in *Abood v. Detroit Board of Education* when it declared that a union could not spend funds for political purposes if nonmembers forced to pay union dues objected to such expenditures; but as a practical matter, Kendrick points out, workers had few protections. Most union officials simply ignored the Court's clear intent. But the foundation kept at it, and in March 1986, in *Chicago Teachers Union v. Hudson*, the Supreme Court ruled unanimously that it is unconstitutional to collect compulsory dues without providing procedural protections that enable workers to prevent use of their dues for political activity and ideological causes.

Thus, as a result of the foundation's efforts, sums up Kendrick, it had won for unionized employees in the government, airlines, and railroads "the right not to pay for union politics and other non-bargaining activities." Whether this right applied to the majority of American workers—the more than 44 million covered by the National Labor Relations Act—remained an open question until *Communications Workers of America v. Beck*. In June 1988, Justice William Brennan, writing for the majority, stated that Congress intended the substantially "identical" authorizations of compulsory unionism in the National Labor Relations Act and the Railway Labor Act "to have the same meaning." Twenty years after its founding, in *Beck*, the National Right to Work Legal Defense Foundation had won for all employees the constitutional right "to stop the use of forced dues for political causes and candidates they had no wish to support."

So far, the foundation has provided free legal aid to about 20,000 individual workers and has assisted more than 368,000 employees through class actions while winning or settling favorably nearly 2,000 cases in federal and state courts and administrative agencies. It is a remarkable and unequalled record of accomplishment in American law. Reed Larson, the man primarily responsible for this record, stepped down in April 2003 as president of the foundation and the National Right to Work Committee; he was succeeded by Mark Mix, who had served with Larson at the foundation for 17 years.

In order to challenge union leaders and their political patrons directly on the issue of corruption, in 1997, the National Legal and Policy Center launched the Organized Labor Accountability Project. The Center was started in 1991 by Kenneth Boehm and Peter Flaherty to promote ethics in public life through litigation, research, and public education. The center exposes union corruption and seeks to influence policymakers in the executive and legislative branches of the federal government.

In the more receptive climate of the George W. Bush administration, the center proposed an overhaul of the LM-2 financial disclosure forms that the nation's wealthiest unions must file with the Department of Labor. Labor Secretary Elaine Chao acted on the proposal, and the new disclosure rules are the first tightening of requirements in 40 years. Another challenge to the alliance of union leaders and political figures, Kendrick says, is coming from the Landmark Legal Foundation, which took aim in June 2000 at the powerful National Education Association. Landmark filed formal complaints with the Internal Revenue Service and the Federal Election Commission against the NEA for failing to comply fully with federal tax and campaign laws. At issue were tens of millions of dollars derived from members' tax-exempt dues that it had spent on unreported political activities. The Labor Department has also initiated an investigation—again at Landmark's request—into the NEA's compliance with federal regulations requiring full disclosure by unions of the use of union membership dues for political purposes. In November 2003, NEA president Reg Weaver admitted that the IRS had informed the teachers union that it would conduct an audit of its finances.

All these advances, concludes Kendrick, are but interim steps toward the fundamental objective of the National Right to Work Legal Defense Foundation, the National Legal and Policy Center, and similar groups. As worker Harry Beck puts it, "Until Congress repeals or the High Court overturns the federal sanction of compulsory dues, workers will not have their full freedoms."

Following the Money

Without hundreds of millions of dollars in annual grants from the nation's largest foundations, says Mark R. Levin in Chapter 9, liberal legal groups like the American Civil Liberties Union and People for the American Way would be "little more than shadows in the wilderness." Ironically, foundations such as Ford, W. K. Kellogg, and John D. and Catherine T. MacArthur were started by individuals who never intended that their fortunes would be used to "undermine the economic system and social institutions that fostered their entrepreneurial success." In fact, six of the top ten grant-making foundations in America give tens of millions of dollars each year to the ACLU, NAACP Legal Defense and Education Fund, Natural Resources Defense Council, Environmental Defense Fund, National Organization for Women, World Wildlife Fund, and similar groups.

In contrast, freedom-based public interest law organizations like the Landmark Legal Foundation, Pacific Legal Foundation, Center for Individual Rights, and other groups mentioned in this history are obliged to counter the liberal activists with far fewer resources and far less money. This "David and Goliath disparity," Levin asserts, makes the record of the freedom-based movement all the more impressive—including such victories as the Clarence Thomas nomination to the Supreme Court; the Milwaukee and Cleveland school voucher cases; the Wilkinsburg, Pennsylvania, privatization case; the 2000 presidential election; and the John Ashcroft nomination to be attorney general.

A continuing strength of the freedom-based public interest law movement is its firm commitment to the Constitution, including the much-misinterpreted Commerce Clause. Case law about interstate commerce since the New Deal era, as John C. Eastman points out in Chapter 10, has given Congress almost unlimited power to "regulate virtually anything it chooses to regulate." In 1978, Harvard law professor Laurence Tribe conceded that "The Supreme Court has ... largely abandoned any effort to articulate and enforce internal limits on congressional power." Nevertheless, says Eastman, pro-freedom public interest law organizations and public policy research groups set out to restore the original understanding of the Commerce Clause and to revive some sense of limits on "the awesome power of the federal government."

In the field of scholarship, starting in the early 1970s, The Heritage Foundation, the Claremont Institute, the Reason Foundation, the Cato Institute, and the Federalist Society published studies and held seminars and conferences on the ideas of private property and limited government as articulated by the Founders of the Republic. They emphasized that, for Supreme Court Chief Justice John Marshall and his colleagues, the notion that the power to regulate commerce among the states also included the power to regulate all other kinds of business activity was completely foreign. This understanding—the original understanding—of the Commerce Clause continued for nearly a century and a half until *Wickard v. Filburn* in 1942.

Leading the litigation charge for the pro-freedom public interest law movement, Eastman says, was the Pacific Legal Foundation, which began some 20 years of work to reinstate the original intent of the Commerce Clause. Other groups that helped along the way were the Southeastern Legal Foundation, the Mountain States Legal Foundation, the Texas Justice Foundation, the Center for Individual Rights, the Washington Legal Foundation, the Cato Institute, the Institute for Justice, Defenders of Property Rights, and the Center for Constitutional Jurisprudence.

Finally, in *United States v. Lopez*, the Supreme Court struck down a federal law on Commerce Clause grounds. Yet the lower courts continued uniformly to reject Commerce Clause challenges to federal regulatory power. The showdown, Eastman writes, came in *United States v. Morrison* when the Fourth Circuit held that the Violence Against Women Act exceeded Congress's Commerce Clause power and the Supreme Court agreed to consider the case. Dozens of briefs representing hundreds of organizations were filed on each side.

Urging the Supreme Court to reverse the Fourth Circuit and uphold the Violence Against Women Act were the Association of Trial Lawyers of America; the Bar Association of the City of New York; the American Association of University Women; the American Federation of State, County and Municipal Employees; a coalition of 100 law professors led by Yale Law's Bruce Ackerman; and 36 states and the Commonwealth of Puerto Rico. Supporting the Fourth Circuit and the original intent of the Commerce Clause were the State of Alabama (represented by its Attorney General William Pryor, later nominated to the 11th Circuit Court of Appeals, and Jeff Sutton, later confirmed to the Sixth Circuit Court of Appeals); several public policy institutions; and a handful of public interest law firms, including the Center for Individual Rights (representing the respondent in the case), the Claremont Institute Center for Constitutional Jurisprudence, the Institute for Justice, the Cato Institute (led by Roger Pilon), and the Pacific Legal Foundation.

By a vote of 5 to 4, the Supreme Court rejected the attempt to marginalize *Lopez* and declared that the Violence Against Women Act had nothing to do with commerce and was not a proper exercise of Congress's Commerce Clause power.

Nevertheless, concludes Eastman, the federal government persists in defending, and the lower courts persist in refusing to add any teeth to, federal regulatory policy about interstate commerce. In the area of environmental law, it remains to be seen whether the Supreme Court is ready to fully apply *Lopez* and the Founders' original view of the Commerce Clause. The proponents of unlimited federal power keep pushing their envelope, but increasingly they are being met and bested by the pro-freedom public interest law movement.

They Also Serve

Non-litigating organizations such as the Federalist Society, the National Legal Center for the Public Interest, the Cato Institute's Center for Constitutional Studies, and The Heritage Foundation's Center for Legal and Judicial Studies contribute significantly to the pro-freedom legal movement. The Federalist Society promotes freedom-based ideas in the academy, the judiciary, and private practice. There are more than 200 chapters (145 at law schools, 60 for lawyers); there are publications such as the prestigious *Harvard Journal of Law and Public Policy*, read widely by members of the federal and state judiciary; and there are such creative initiatives as the Pro Bono Resource Center, which facilitates free legal aid through a sophisticated computer system. Under president Eugene Meyer, the Federalist Society has helped to identify law students and lawyers that share constitutional principles and to identify issues calling for litigation.

The Cato Institute started the Center for Constitutional Studies in 1989 to advance the basic idea that the Constitution protects liberty through limited government and that the judiciary must actively secure that legal order. Under Roger Pilon, Cato's vice president for legal affairs, the center has published numerous books, studies, monographs, and op-ed newspaper essays; since 1998, for example, it has sold or distributed 3 million copies of a pocket Declaration of Independence and Constitution. The center has filed *amicus* briefs and in the fall of 2002 began producing the *Cato Supreme Court Review*, an annual review of the term just ended. The Center for Constitutional Studies, says Pilon, works with colleagues in the academy and elsewhere to "change the climate of ideas" so that litigation advancing limited constitutional government will be successful.

Chaired by former Attorney General Edwin Meese III, The Heritage Foundation's Center for Legal and Judicial Studies brings together at regular meetings the CEOs of the nation's leading freedom-based public interest legal groups. Such meetings facilitate cooperation such as the filing of *amicus* briefs in key cases. Under Director Todd Gaziano, the center sponsors a Supreme Court Advocacy program that includes e-mail alerts, *amicus curiae* brief conferences, and mock oral argument sessions. The center has an active communications program that places its scholars, such as Senior Legal Research Fellow Paul Rosenzweig, and other experts on television and radio.

This history proves that the pro-freedom legal movement has made a decisive difference through its leadership role in such landmark Supreme Court decisions as:

Widmar v. Vincent (1981): religious liberty.

Adarand Constructors, Inc. v. Peña (1995): affirmative action.

Nollan v. California Coastal Commission (1987): property rights.

Communications Workers of America v. Beck (1988): workers' rights.

Keller v. State Bar of California (1990): compelled speech.

United States v. Lopez (1995): Commerce Clause.

Dolan v. City of Tigard (1994): economic liberty.

Boy Scouts of America v. Dale (2000): freedom of speech.

Zelman v. Simmons-Harris (2002): school choice.

As for the future, the freedom-based public interest law movement will strive as it has for more than 30 years to bring justice to the people by safeguarding their liberties and protecting the original meaning of that indispensable document of our freedom—the U.S. Constitution.

---

[1] James Q. Wilson, *American Government* (Lexington, Mass.: D. C. Heath & Company, 1980), p. 398.

[2] William H. Rehnquist, essay in Mark W. Cannon and David M. O'Brien, eds., *Views from the Bench: The Judiciary and Constitutional Politics* (New York: Chatham House Publishers, 1985).

[3] William J. Brennan, Jr., essay in *Views from the Bench*.

[4] Lee Edwards, *Freedom's College: The History of Grove City College* (Washington, D.C.: Regnery Publishing, 2000), p. 80.

[5] Charles K. Rowley, *The Right to Justice: The Political Economy of Legal Services in the United States* (Brookfield, Vt.: Edward Elgar Publishing, 1992), p. 7.

[6] See Chapter 6 in David Bollier, *Citizen Action and Other Big Ideas: A History of Ralph Nader and the Modern Consumer Movement* (Washington, D.C.: Center for Study of Responsive Law, 1989).

[7] A favorite formulation of Ralph Nader. See *ibid.*

[8] Rowley, *The Right to Justice*, p. 4.

[9] See Kenneth F. Boehm, "Thwarting the Will of Congress: How the Legal Services Corporation Evaded, Diluted and Ignored Reform," testimony before the Subcommittee on Commercial and Administrative Law, Committee on the Judiciary, U.S. House of Representatives, February 28, 2002.

[10] F. LaGard Smith, *ACLU: The Devil's Advocate, The Seduction of Civil Liberties in America* (Colorado Springs, Colo.: Marcon Publishers, 1996), p. v.

[11] *Ibid.*, pp. 235–234.

[12] Lou Cannon, *Governor Reagan: His Rise to Power* (New York: Public Affairs, 2003), p. 359.

[13] "How Rehnquist Changed America," *Time*, June 30, 2003.

CHAPTER 2

Life, Liberty, and Property Rights

Ronald A. Zumbrun

Public interest law in the United States is many decades old. As of 1989, there were more than 158 liberal public interest law firms functioning within the United States, employing over 900 lawyers and expending over $120 million annually. In addition, a large portion of the over $300 million appropriated annually through the federal Legal Services Corporation was directed toward public interest law-type activities rather than direct legal representation of low-income individuals. There also were state bar and local legal aid programs directing a significant amount of money to these efforts. Of particular significance are statutorily authorized attorney fees available only to groups litigating "in the public interest."

When the Pacific Legal Foundation was incorporated in Sacramento, California, on March 5, 1973, it was described by the American Bar Association as the first public interest law firm in the United States that was philosophically other than liberal to radical.[1] This left a lot of room within which to operate.

Where the Pacific Legal Foundation differed from the other groups was that PLF was formed to defend and enhance individ-

ual and economic freedom in our country by litigating and participating in administrative proceedings to support the free enterprise system, private property rights, and concepts of limited
government. Beginning in 1975, other non-liberal public interest
law firms began to form in other regions of the United States,
modeled in part after the Pacific Legal Foundation. However,
each organization was unique in nature and personality. Some
organizations were single-issue efforts, while most dealt with a
broad spectrum of interests.

The Pacific Legal Foundation was an outgrowth of California
Governor Ronald Reagan's highly successful welfare reform program, which was conceived during the fall of 1970 and implemented beginning in January 1971. While the welfare reform program
achieved success both for the recipient and the taxpayer, it was
implemented under considerable controversy and confrontation.[2]

Attacks on the Reagan program were spearheaded by welfare
rights organizations, legal aid societies, social worker unions, certain elements of the legislature, and numerous public interest law
firms. It became quite apparent to those supporting the reform
program that there was a serious imbalance within the public
interest law field. It appeared that no one was litigating in support of our basic system of government: the free enterprise system, traditional private property rights, and a balanced approach
to weighing economic, social, *and* environmental concerns.

During mid-1972, there were several discussions concerning
the need for a new type of nonprofit public interest law firm. The
first occurred among members of the welfare reform legal team,
which involved a group of governmental trial attorneys who
assisted in the development, implementation, and defense of the
welfare reform effort.[3] The next conversations involved the California Chamber of Commerce and Roy A. Green, instrumental in
developing public support for California's welfare reform program; James M. Hall, secretary of the Human Relations Agency

of the state of California, who had overall responsibility for the welfare reform effort; Robert Carleson, California state welfare director; and Edwin Meese III, executive secretary to Governor Reagan. As a result of those conversations, support was generated for a new effort in public interest law.

At the same time, the late John Simon Fluor had been discussing his frustrations and concerns with William French Smith, senior partner of the Gibson, Dunn & Crutcher law firm (and subsequently attorney general of the United States), regarding the environmental movement. Of particular concern to Fluor was the delay of the Alaska Pipeline project; the enjoining of the Mineral King development in Kern County, California; and certain delays in offshore drilling in the Gulf of Mexico. Smith, who was participating in the effort to create a new type of public interest law firm, suggested that Fluor also become involved.

In January 1973, a group of concerned individuals, including a leading attorney and civic leader from each of the six geographical regions in California, met in San Francisco to discuss the possible formation of a pro-freedom public interest law firm. A potential board of trustees was designated, and Ronald A. Zumbrun was requested to develop a formal policy concept document. The policy concept was submitted in writing to the proposed board of trustees on February 1, 1973. It was then presented orally at a February 8 meeting in San Francisco and adopted. The decision was made to incorporate. The 53-page document included objectives, the basic concept, the mode of implementation, areas of interest, and operating policy for the proposed organization—to be named the Pacific Legal Foundation.

On March 5, 1973, the Pacific Legal Foundation was incorporated. John Simon Fluor was elected chairman of the board.[4] Eleven of the first individuals to join the foundation staff were all part of the Reagan welfare reform team.[5] A proposed budget of $117,000 was designated for the first 10 months of operation.

The foundation received its tax-exempt status from the Internal Revenue Service under Section 501(c)(3) of the Internal Revenue Code and began its litigation activities in June 1973.

The freedom-based public interest law effort in 1989 entered its 17th year of activity. However, the funding and litigation staffing of the pro-free enterprise effort was dwarfed by that of the traditional liberal legal groups. For example, during 1988, the pro-freedom groups had fewer than 50 litigators and total budgets of less than $11 million. Their philosophical opponents continued at their high levels of over 900 attorneys and $120 million annually, thanks to the Legal Services Corporation and other legal aid-type money. Also, the liberal groups continued to be funded by handsome awards of attorney fees by the courts and by state bar associations, which provided substantial funding. For example, the California Legislature passed legislation that assured over $15.5 million during 1988.

The significance of traditional liberal public interest law groups cannot be overstated. Time and again, judicial activism has thwarted or redirected the will of the majority as expressed by legislative bodies and carried out by the executive branch. As judges became more willing to make law rather than just interpret law, the impact grew even greater. However, slowly but surely, the freedom-based non-liberal groups established their ability to neutralize their opposing public interest groups as well as to take the offensive and establish their own agenda with the courts and regulatory bodies. It is interesting to note that in 1989, the number of attorneys involved in freedom-based public interest law was essentially the same number as comprised the liberal movement in 1969, just before their big expansion during the 1970s.

The Practice of Public Interest Law

All public interest law firms are regulated by the Internal Revenue Service and are eligible for a Section 501(c)(3) charitable tax deduction under the Internal Revenue Code. They specialize in precedent-setting legal activities, are not allowed to charge for their services, and exist to provide representation for interests that would not otherwise be before the courts.

The practice of freedom-based public interest law is one of the most challenging types of litigation for an attorney. It involves issues that are on the cutting edge of the law, destined to go to the highest levels of the court system. At the same time, it usually involves litigating against heavily staffed and funded governmental agencies and, often, heavily staffed and aggressive radical legal organizations. One's credibility is constantly being challenged, and liberal groups go to great lengths to try to destroy the efforts of those who support our basic system of government and believe in free enterprise, limited government, and private property rights.

The practice of public interest law is further complicated by judicial activism wherein courts act as legislators rather than jurists. Judicial activism tends to be practiced by the more liberal members of the judiciary and is frowned upon by the more conservative, strict interpretation-type judges. This creates difficulties for freedom-based lawyers, who are subjected to court sanctions and attacks in the mass media.

This was especially true in the late 1970s and early 1980s when the judiciary had been appointed primarily by President Jimmy Carter and such governors as California's Jerry Brown. As a result, the courts were dominated by extreme judicial activists. The risks, however, have diminished significantly, partly due to the success of the freedom-based public interest law firms and the changing attitude of the judiciary toward judicial activism. This change allowed cases to be brought and procedures to be tested that previously would have been too risky to attempt, even though the law was on the side of the proponent.

The win/loss record of a public interest law firm is always of interest to donors, but it is really a meaningless assessment. Many of the public interest law firms pride themselves on an excellent win/loss ratio. What is important, however, is what was won, because what was lost probably would have been lost anyway. The focus should be on what has been positively accomplished.

Some public interest law firms function under the code of conduct and ethical standards of the established bar. In other words, if you can't win by the rules, then perhaps you shouldn't be in the game. Some groups, however, function outside of the establishment. This is particularly true of more radical liberal organizations. Members of the freedom-based law movement believe that since they are trying to support our system of government, they should play by the rules of that system.

The pro-free enterprise public interest law movement initially suffered difficulties similar to those of the rest of the nonprofit world. Fund raising and self-survival often dominated program goals. However, most participants in the conservative public interest law movement who have litigated successfully in the trenches have a market value far exceeding their salary. These individuals, most of whom gain no recognition outside their organization and local bar association, are true heroes who have made a substantial difference in public interest law.

Private Property Rights

The area of land use litigation is one of the most difficult for freedom-based public interest litigators. It is full of legal land mines set by government and the courts.

After two years of litigating successfully in other areas of the law,[6] the Pacific Legal Foundation felt it necessary to establish a specialized land use section. The foundation was fortunate in attracting the services of a successful land use private practitioner[7] to head this effort. Over the years, the foundation became known as an expert in the field.[8]

Unfortunately, the foundation's land use efforts were increasingly frustrated by the attitudes of the state and federal courts.

Four times, PLF was involved in cases accepted by the U.S. Supreme Court only to have them dismissed on technical grounds following oral argument.[9] Accordingly, the high court did not reach the merits of the important land use cases it had chosen to hear. In early 1986, the foundation began to consider getting out of the land use field and leaving these policy decisions to the state legislature and Congress.

Prior to November 1986, the trend of constitutional interpretation, or the lack thereof, had been particularly onerous in the areas of government regulation and property rights law. The framers of our Constitution believed in limited government and that the right to own and reasonably use private property was a basic freedom. These concepts form a cornerstone of our Constitution. Over the centuries, the courts have been the primary defender of these freedoms.

However, beginning in the 1930s, the courts became less inclined and less motivated to restrict government and defend private property rights. Government took property through regulation, and the courts would not provide any financial remedy to the property owner. States used the power of eminent domain where there was no public use envisioned for the property being acquired. Activist jurists and organizations used concepts like rent control and environmental protection to change our basic economic system. An exaction game evolved, in which the challenge was to figure out what the government could take as a condition for issuing a license or a permit to which the applicant was otherwise entitled.

The process became particularly rough if you lived on the California coast. In fact, qualifying for a permit sometimes cost up to one-half of your entire property! If you were "lucky" enough to live in Santa Monica, you might have had to make a $5,000 contribution to a special "cultural fund," or 10 percent of your gross profits. If you refused to play the game, you were faced with a worse fate—years of expensive litigation and the corresponding loss of use of your property as you undertook the fight. If the permit sought to protect your property from "acts of God" such as storm, fire, or flood, waiting meant you lost your property anyway when the anticipated event occurred. States such as New York and Texas used these events as their primary springboard for government confiscation.

It was very difficult to challenge this process in court. Not only were the courts unsympathetic, but there was a great unwillingness by permit or license seekers to sue. It was more economical to pay the exaction than to fight city hall.

A primary criticism of the Supreme Court at that time was that it tended to emphasize the power of government over the rights of the individual. It talked in terms of upholding states' rights and expressed the belief that government closest to the people was the best government. However, in case after case, the Court gave such a broad interpretation to the power of government, rather than to its responsibility to the governed, that the rights and freedoms of the individual were subrogated to the power of the majority. This was both a highly dangerous course to travel and a flawed view of states' rights. The power of government, wherever placed, will not work within our constitutional framework unless it is an exercise of responsibility rather than a tyranny of the majority.

The Sleeping Giant Awakes

Beginning in late 1986, there was an abrupt change in the direction of public interest law. First, the Supreme Court took jurisdiction of a number of individual rights cases—particularly in the government regulation and land use fields. These included the issue of whether there should be a compensation remedy for a regulatory taking of private property, whether the exaction game is unconstitutional, whether a landlord in a rent control district can be denied a rent increase solely because the tenant is suffering financial hardship, whether innocent private parties can be forced to pay for the cleanup of toxic pollution caused by government negligence, and whether prohibitions against racial discrimination apply to all races.

Just as significant as the Supreme Court's reassertion of its role as a defender of individual freedoms were the ramifications of the November 1986 judicial election in California, wherein three California Supreme Court justices were not re-elected. This was the beginning of the demise of judicial activism in that state as well as in other jurisdictions that got the message: The public, by a 2 to 1 margin, rejected the jurists who were perceived as judicial lawmakers rather than interpreters.

The California election was important because it demonstrated that the public would not tolerate judges who rewrite law under the guise of interpreting law. The reaction was not merely a partisan political phenomenon. The 2 to 1 margin of defeat was not a question of Republicans versus Democrats: The latter are the majority in California. Even 64 percent of the judges in California who responded to a *Los Angeles Times* poll voted against at least one of the Supreme Court justices. Fifty-nine percent of the judges who described themselves as moderate and 24 percent of the judges who described themselves as liberal voted against at least one of the justices.

The ousted jurists erred in usurping the power of the legislature and of the people to make law. Having given up their judicial independence, they were treated by the public as any other politician would be treated.

The next historical event occurred in 1987 when the U.S. Supreme Court decided Pacific Legal Foundation's *Nollan v. California Coastal Commission* case and *First English Evangelical Lutheran Church of Glendale v. County of Los Angeles*. These cases involved an individual church and an individual family pitted against government. In *First Church*, the Supreme Court held that there is a compensation remedy when government by regulation deprives an individual of the use of private property. The decision, authored by Chief Justice William Rehnquist, went further and found a right to interim damages for government-caused delays or when government chooses not to proceed after the court has found that a taking has occurred.

In *Nollan*, authored by Justice Antonin Scalia, the Court held that the exaction game was over and that the California Coastal Commission could not require Patrick and Marilyn Nollan to dedicate one-third of their property to the state as a condition of receiving a permit to rebuild their home. The Court declared that the commission's practice was "an out-and-out plan of extortion." Government may no longer impose exactions and conditions on permits or licenses where the individual otherwise has a right. This ruling applies to all governmental agencies nationwide that issue permits or licenses.

The Supreme Court in *Nollan* also changed its practice of giving full deference to government and presuming governmental regularity. Instead, the Court held that government regulations and exactions are to be subjected to "strict scrutiny." Thus, the power balance has adjusted and the individual has the right to ask the courts to look behind government action and scrutinize strictly. While government technically does not have the burden of proof, under the strict scrutiny rule the practical effect is a shifting of that burden.

The Court also set up numerous other tests for judging the validity of a permit condition, including the requirement that government must show that its actions substantially further a legitimate governmental purpose. The result is that governmental agencies with confiscatory or other unacceptable intents are out of business.[10] In the future, they will have to pay for what they take. Certainty and fairness are to be restored in the government regulatory process. In the meantime, there is much work to be done and opportunities galore for the freedom-based public interest litigator.

Nollan is widely considered to be the most important land use case in at least the past 65 years. It has led to a series of victories and precedents, as well as a renewed attention to private property rights.[11]

Other significant judicial trends in public interest law include the Court's decisions indicating that prohibitions against racial discrimination apply to all races. Access to jobs, housing, public contracts, education, and other such opportunities will not be based on race no matter what government decrees or what race, creed, religion, or national origin is in vogue. Major changes also have occurred in the areas of federalism and states' rights, religious freedom, and basic individual and economic freedoms.

The Future of Public Interest Law

As stated by California Chief Justice Malcolm Lucas while speaking to a group of Pacific Legal Foundation supporters shortly after his confirmation in March 1987:

> [Y]ou should not assume that the new court will so readily overturn or reexamine prior decisions having an adverse effect upon the search for justice. These former decisions will remain comfortably in place until someone has the ambition, in the context of a particular appeal, to raise the question of whether a reexamination of the underlying principles may be appropriate. I suggest therefore that your Foundation will continue to play an important role and perhaps an even more useful and appreciated role than ever before in the development and reshaping of the civil and criminal law....

It is up to the freedom-based law movement and its allies to seize the offensive and take advantage of the opportunities at hand. The next 30 years could be comparable to the 1970s explosion of liberal public interest activists, which resulted in a growth from 50 to over 900 liberal public interest lawyers in less than 15 years.

It is clear from the preceding history that there is more opportunity than ever before to use the courts to preserve and enhance individual and economic freedom. Mainstream America believes in the basic philosophy of the freedom-based public interest law movement and has the capacity to provide the necessary funding. It remains for the movement to help the silent majority understand that the time to help is now.

---

[1] American Bar Association, *Consortium on Legal Services and the Public*, Vol. 1, No. 2 (October, 1973).

[2] For a thorough description of the California welfare reform effort, see Ronald A. Zumbrun, Raymond Momboisse, and John H. Findley, "Welfare Reform: California Meets the Challenge," *Pacific Law Journal*, Vol. 4, No. 2 (July 1973).

[3] The first discussion occurred at an annual statewide county counsel convention in Monterey, California, between Ronald A. Zumbrun, deputy director-legal affairs, California State Department of Social Welfare; Richard Parslow, Orange County District Attorney's Office; and Mike Barber of the Sacramento County District Attorney's Office.

[4] Si Fluor was an inspirational leader who took individual responsibility to raise the funds for the seed money necessary for PLF to open its doors. His stature and vision were a key to PLF's early success.

[5] These individuals included Ron Zumbrun, legal director; attorneys Ray Momboisse, John Findley, Dick Parslow, Dave Todd, Bob Best, and Tom Hookano; founding trustee Jim Hall; Roy Green, executive vice president; and secretaries Marilyn Carruthers and Barbara Hartsfield. Shelton Olson was also part of the original team responsible for fiscal and administrative matters. During her 20-year tenure at PLF, she soon advanced to become executive vice president.

[6] There were no final judgments against PLF during its first two years. This was important since opposing groups and attorneys and certain members of the media were forced to deal with PLF's track record rather than their own hyperbole.

[7] Donald Pach, followed by Bob Best and Ed Connor.

[8] PLF's land use experts also included John Findley, Jim Burling, Rob Rivett, Orrin Finch, R. S. Radford, Tim Bittle, Hal Hughes, and Darlene Ruiz. Tom Caso is the current general counsel and senior vice president.

[9] Each case involved the issue of whether government must pay compensation for a regulatory taking of private property.

[10] It is a primary goal of the freedom-based movement to make sure that this occurs.

[11] This is particularly true in the legal profession, as the *Nollan* case is included in every law school's property law case book and is a subject in final exams as well as in the bar exam.

CHAPTER 3

School Choice: Triumph for Freedom

Clint Bolick

O f all the victories of the pro-freedom public interest law movement, none may have greater real-world impact—and none may ever be sweeter—than the ruling in *Zelman v. Simmons-Harris*,[1] which lifted the federal constitutional cloud from school choice. In that case, the Supreme Court took a major step forward in vindicating the promise of *Brown v. Board of Education* and its sacred promise of educational opportunities.

When it came time to pop the champagne corks, it was conservative and libertarian public interest lawyers and their mostly minority and low-income clients who were celebrating, while left-wing advocacy groups went home to sulk. For that reason, the school choice victory was not only a landmark legal decision, but also a milestone in the evolution, maturation, and effectiveness of the pro-freedom public interest law movement.[2]

The battle started small. In 1990, when I was director of the Washington, D.C.-based Landmark Legal Foundation Center for Civil Rights, I read a short article in *The Washington Times* describing a small program that the Wisconsin Legislature had just enacted. The Milwaukee Parental Choice Program would allow up to 1,000 low-income children to use a portion of their state education funds as full payment of tuition in nonsectarian private schools.

Having become a lawyer only after detouring from my planned career as a schoolteacher, I had long supported the concept of school choice as a vital part of the solution to the woes of inner-city public schooling. I recognized that the Milwaukee program, regardless of its size, was an epic achievement in education reform.

For the first time in American history, power over basic educational opportunities would be transferred from bureaucrats to parents; and also for the first time, public schools would have to compete for low-income children and the funds now at their disposal. The first brick had been removed from the Berlin Wall of monopoly public schooling.

For those reasons, the education establishment fought back. In addition to the lawsuit filed by the union and its allies challenging the program under the state constitution, the head of the Department of Public Instruction, Bert Grover, imposed a blizzard of regulations on private schools in an effort to sentence the program to death by bureaucratic strangulation. We had to intervene on behalf of parents and children to defend the program alongside the state; then we had to turn around and sue the state to remove the regulations. And we had to win both battles over the course of a single summer in order for the program to start in fall 1990.

We won that battle, but many more followed. When I first called to congratulate the Milwaukee program's sponsor, a black Democrat and former welfare mother, State Representative Polly Williams, I asked whether she was ready for the lawsuit. In words that proved painfully immortal, she said, "What lawsuit?" Over the next 12 years, my colleagues and I would litigate 16 school choice lawsuits from Puerto Rico to California—with more to follow in the aftermath of *Zelman*.

When William "Chip" Mellor and I launched the Institute for Justice in 1991, we vowed to defend every school choice program until their survival was assured, proclaiming, "If you have a school choice program, you have a lawyer!" Among others, we filed lawsuits seeking a voucher remedy for educational deprivations under the state constitutions in California and Illinois; we defended against a second challenge to the Milwaukee program when it was expanded in 1995 to include religious schools; we defended voucher programs in Puerto Rico, Ohio, and Florida; and we defended scholarship and tuition tax credits in Arizona and Illinois.[3] Finally we prevailed in the U.S. Supreme Court in *Zelman* on the federal Establishment Clause issue, removing the primary constitutional obstacle. Yet many constitutional challenges still remain at the state level.

Along the way, my colleagues and I learned a great number of lessons, many of which may be helpful to the broader pro-freedom public interest law movement.

Seizing the Offensive

Our posture in most of the school choice cases was unusual for public interest lawyers: Instead of suing the government, we served as intervenor-defendants on the side of the state. From those experiences, we gained several important insights. First, a significant, largely untapped niche exists for pro-freedom public interest groups to defend reform legislation. One might reasonably measure the impact of reform legislation by whether it is challenged in court. If it is not challenged, it probably doesn't amount to much, because serious pro-market reforms almost always cause pain to entrenched special-interest groups. By intervening, we can protect the interests of the intended beneficiaries of the reform.[4]

Second, it is important not to leave the legal defense of the programs to state attorneys general. Many of them are skillful and dedicated, and it is important to establish a good working relationship, but attorneys general are subject to political aspirations and pressures.

Often, the office changes hands in the middle of litigation. Moreover, attorneys general often have an institutional interest in avoiding provocative legal tactics, such as moving to recuse biased judges. Only by intervening as parties can we make sure that someone is focused exclusively and passionately on defending the program.

The best way to defend a program is by investing legal resources in its creation. We have counseled hundreds of legislators and activists in an effort to legally "bullet proof" school choice legislation. Most of the legislative efforts failed; but by involving ourselves from the start, we knew that we would have the most defensible possible legislation if it passed and that we would be utterly familiar with it. Further, in that process we established relationships that would enable us to hit the ground running once lawsuits were filed.

In Florida, we began working with Jeb Bush and other school choice activists four years before he was elected governor. After he was elected, we worked with Governor Bush and his team to fashion constitutionally sound legislation in accord with the governor's campaign promises. Before the bill was even signed, the team was in place and we were prepared for the legal onslaught.

Intervention has its downsides. Though we were able to present oral argument at every level in every case until the U.S. Supreme Court, we always played a secondary role in court. Typically, however, we had the same number of pages in our briefs, we were able to pursue separate legal strategies when necessary, we had the opportunity to offer evidence, and we were able to supplement our litigation with activities outside the courtroom. And in court, we were able to play the relief pitcher role, focusing on the human dimension and addressing issues that had presented difficulty to our co-counsel.

Honing Legal Strategy

Over the course of the 12 years leading to *Zelman*, we authored about 75 briefs in school choice cases. Repetition often leads to formulaic approaches, and we were determined never to let our advocacy grow stale. We approached each brief afresh. As we began anticipating a U.S. Supreme Court case, we hosted a gathering of Establishment Clause scholars at the Jefferson Hotel in Washington, D.C. Because the hotel is located across the street from the National Education Association, we dubbed it the "Shadow of the Beast Conference."

There, the scholars dissected our briefs and gave us advice on how best to fashion the argument in the Supreme Court. We also discussed ancillary strategies. By conferring long before a case was accepted for review, we were able to craft at leisure a sound approach. The strategy helped guide us even in trial court proceedings, as we had considered what evidence would be necessary for the record on appeal.

The theme that emerged from the conference was that we had to characterize the case as being about education, not religion. If the other side succeeded in making the fight about legal abstractions, they would win; but if we could make clear that the case was really about educational opportunities for children who desperately needed them, we would have a fighting chance. That theme permeated both our legal tactics and our rhetoric.

When we reached the Supreme Court, we were faced with the pleasant prospect of having three party briefs (one for the state, one for another set of intervenors, and one for the Institute for Justice). Rather than duplicate the solid legal arguments of our co-parties, we filed a "Brandeis brief," focusing on the record and equities. As a legal hook, we took the Establishment Clause "primary effect" test, which all parties agreed governed the case, and translated it into a real-world standard.

That allowed us to talk about the crisis of inner-city education, the emergency in the Cleveland public schools, and the benefits of the school choice program. We blended in social science data and parent affidavits. We also repeatedly invoked *Brown v. Board of Education*, provoking a hysterical response from the NAACP Legal Defense and Education Fund that had the effect of highlighting that very argument. Looking at the Court's opinion, it seems evident that those arguments influenced the successful outcome.

Likewise, we helped coordinate *amicus* briefs so that they would complement the parties' arguments. (In some cases, they also helpfully made the parties' arguments appear more moderate by comparison.) Working with The Heritage Foundation and Kenneth Starr, among others, we helped prepare the advocates for oral argument. The touchstone was constant communication and coordination.

A crucial lesson here was to make sure that every contributor to the legal effort, and every page in our combined briefs, made a distinctive point or reinforced important points in a different way. Every page and every minute counts.

Nontraditional Alliances

Every major school choice program, from Milwaukee to Cleveland to Florida to Colorado to Washington, D.C., was made possible only with bipartisan support. Likewise, the legal team reflected the cross-ideological support for school choice.

Inherently, the defense of school choice combines libertarian or conservative lawyers with low-income parents. This nontraditional alliance characterizes much of the Institute for Justice's work, not only in school choice, but also in the areas of economic liberty and property rights. It makes sense as a priority for the pro-freedom public interest law movement because, if we truly believe in expanding freedom, we should make common cause with the people in our society who are least free. The alliance of free-market groups with low-income people makes for a powerful political force and helps in the courtroom as well.

In each case, we worked with local free-market policy groups, who helped provide invaluable infrastructure support, but also with liberal pro-school choice community leaders. In Milwaukee, for instance, not only did we work with Polly Williams, but we also worked with Mayor John Norquist, former Milwaukee Public Schools Superintendent Howard Fuller, and school board member John Gardner. All of them gave the legal effort enormous bipartisan credibility. Working with Gardner, a professional labor organizer who previously worked for Cesar Chavez, was especially enlightening. Liberals traditionally have been effective organizers, and we hope that some of Gardner's acumen rubbed off on the Institute for Justice.

As we approached the Supreme Court, we endeavored to diversify the legal team as well. A number of liberal legal academics had expressed the belief that school choice was constitutional. We helped bring a number of them, along with conservative scholars, onto an *amicus* brief authored by former Berkeley Law School Dean Jesse Choper. Norquist and New York Mayor Rudy Giuliani co-authored a brief urging the Court to sustain school choice as a vital policy option. Former Clinton administration solicitor Walter Dellinger aided the oral argument preparation team.

Our view was that the broader the team, the more likely we would be to communicate effectively with each member of the Court. An ecumenical approach to litigation seems essential to the public interest legal enterprise.

Parents Front and Center

A typical lawyer strategy is to keep the client silent and in the background. That won't do for public interest litigation. Our clients are often our best asset, and it is important that they speak for themselves.

At the Institute for Justice, we apply to all our cases a strategy of "the three ize's": personalize, humanize, and dramatize. By *personalize*, we mean making the battle one that focuses on the real lives of real people in David versus Goliath fashion. By *humanize*, we mean invoking the common thread that links our clients with other Americans—in this case, the universal desire among parents to attain the best possible educational opportunities for their children. And by *dramatize*—well, that's pretty obvious: The parents had a compelling story to tell about the horrible schools to which their children were consigned and their hopes for a better future.

So our strategy was to make sure that the parents not only were represented in the courtroom, but also were actually present there. At every hearing, we brought parents and children to court and often held rallies outside the courtroom. At one hearing in the Milwaukee case, the ACLU lawyer moaned, "Here comes Clint and his kids again." The parents and children were also the central focus of our equitable arguments before the court.

At the Wisconsin Supreme Court, our local allies brought 16 busloads of parents and children to rally on the steps of the Capitol. As passionate speeches were delivered and the crowd sang "We Shall Overcome," the union's legal team walked past. Inside the courtroom, the skillful lead lawyer for the National Education Association, Robert Chanin, actually melted down during his argument, announcing that he was tired of being characterized as the man in the black hat and proclaiming that he cared about education, too. It wasn't our side's advocacy that made him lose his cool. It was the unnerving and implicitly accusatory presence of the parents and children.

The Court of Public Opinion

Our belief at the Institute for Justice, urged by our communications team and its talented director, John Kramer, is that we argue in two courts: the court of law and the court of public opinion. Not only do judges read newspapers and watch television, but high-profile cases can be powerfully important teaching tools, galvanizing public support for the cause. Here again, placing the parents front and center helps to make a strong case.

Likewise, in each jurisdiction where we litigate, we have worked with our local allies to facilitate visits by reporters to showcase schools and interviews with representative parents. In the early days of the Milwaukee battle, when Mike Wallace of *60 Minutes* came to town and produced a heart-tugging segment favorable to the school choice program, we knew we were onto something.

In Florida, we were even more aggressive. Once the school choice program passed, we were extremely concerned that the liberal Florida judiciary would enjoin the program before it even started. We had learned that it was vital to make the programs operational as quickly as possible because it is easier for a court to halt a program that hasn't yet started than to wrench children out of good schools. One of our directors generously funded a paid media campaign with advertisements in the state's four leading daily newspapers featuring a photo of our lead clients, a mother and daughter.

The advertisements proclaimed that little Jessica Merkman finally had a chance for a good education—but that the American Civil Liberties Union wanted to take it away. In turn, the ads themselves attracted secondary news and editorial coverage. It is tough to shame the ACLU, but the ads did just that, placing the anti-choice crusaders on the defensive before they left the starting gate. For the first time in school choice litigation, the plaintiffs decided not to seek an injunction. And despite a continuing legal challenge, the Florida opportunity scholarship program continues today, five years later and much larger than the original.

Over the years of litigation, we brought parents and local activists to scores of editorial boards. Eventually, liberal publications such as *The Washington Post, USA Today*, and *The New Republic* came to make crucial endorsements of school choice. Our communications team created a "School Choice Resource Center" on our Web site that could answer every reporter's questions about school choice generally and provide specific cases and programs. Our principal message throughout, echoing our legal strategy, was that the legal debate over school choice was about education, not religion. We repeatedly characterized *Zelman* as "the most important education case since *Brown v. Board of Education*."

The efforts in the court of public opinion culminated, on the day of the Supreme Court argument, in a massive rally that brought in parents and children from all across the nation. It helped that the argument took place on an unusually balmy February day. Our team managed to scope out the crucial territory in front of the Supreme Court while the teachers union, earning a "tardy" for the day, was relegated to a position across the street. The mission was accomplished: On virtually all the evening newscasts, and on nearly all the newspaper front pages the following day, coverage about the court argument was accompanied by parents talking about how important school choice was to them.

The Road Ahead

The resulting legal ruling was an important catalyst for renewed school choice efforts, including in the District of Columbia, but the legal journey was often painful: Along the way, we actually lost many more rounds in court than we won. We learned that perspicacity and stamina are probably the two most important qualities of successful public interest lawyers, and we needed both in abundance.

By keeping our eyes on the long-range goal and doing everything we could think of to achieve it, our allies and we eventually won the most crucial battle. Daunting legal obstacles remain, but the size and breadth of the coalition supporting school choice are growing.

The successful legal battle for school choice—sometimes the result of inspired strategy, other times the product of accident and serendipity—contains many valuable lessons for pro-freedom litigators. In many ways, we are borrowing (and, we hope, improving upon) tactics developed over the decades by liberal public interest litigators.

But we now have an historic opportunity because liberals have abdicated many of the tactics that made them successful, particularly the human dimension of legal advocacy. The denizens of the early days of civil rights, environmental, and consumer litigation must wonder from their graves how the Left managed to find itself in a landmark court battle *against* the interests of inner-city, low-income parents and children. As their cases become increasingly radical and abstract, they are handing us opportunities to remake the policy and legal landscape.

We must seize the opportunity and make common cause with those who are most victimized by the nanny state. Through the powerful tool of strategic litigation, working with nontraditional clients and allies, we can identify the interests of economic outsiders with freedom, and in the process create opportunities for the most truly disadvantaged in our society to earn their share of the American Dream.

As the Left recognized decades ago, and as we are now beginning to appreciate more fully, law is a powerful tool for social change. Those of us who are lucky enough to be pro-freedom litigators have opportunities that are bound only by our passion and imagination. *Carpe diem!*

---

[1] 536 U.S. 639 (2002).

[2] For a more comprehensive discussion of the 12 years of litigation leading up to *Zelman*, see Clint Bolick, *Voucher Wars: Waging the Legal Battle Over School Choice* (Washington, D.C.: Cato Institute, 2002).

[3] At present, we are defending voucher programs in Florida and Colorado and scholarship tax credits in Arizona, and attempting to eliminate religious school exclusion in voucher programs in Vermont and Maine. We also anticipate a legal challenge to the recently enacted Washington, D.C., voucher program.

[4] A good example is the defense of Proposition 209, the California Civil Rights Initiative. The Center for Individual Rights, Pacific Legal Foundation, and the Institute for Justice all played significant roles in defending the measure.

CHAPTER 4

Defending Religious Liberty

Alan E. Sears[1]

On December 8, 1981, a surprised murmur rippled through
the gallery of the Supreme Court as Chief Justice Warren
Burger announced that the justices were handing down
their decision in the important religious liberty case of *Widmar v.
Vincent*. The high court had heard oral arguments in the case only
two months earlier. *Widmar* presented the question whether the
Constitution protected the freedom of speech rights of students at
the University of Missouri-Kansas City to meet on campus for a
weekly evangelical Christian worship service, or whether the Constitution's Establishment Clause required the university to ban
such meetings. No one expected the Supreme Court to hand down
such a major decision in such a short time.

The news for religious liberty was better than many had dared
hope. Justice Lewis Powell announced the lopsided 8 to 1 decision
rejecting the university's extreme "separation of church and state"
defense and strongly endorsing the students' freedom of speech position that entitled them to meet on campus: The government does not
endorse the viewpoints expressed by private groups meeting in
government facilities generally available for all groups. In a

constitutional decision of Copernican magnitude, the Supreme Court in *Widmar* restored the Freedom of Speech Clause to the center of the equal access system, casting aside the Ptolemaic position of the secularists that the "separation of church and state" should rule in all such cases.

Widmar was a big win for the growing religious liberty movement, begun primarily by evangelical Protestants and other Christians to fight encroaching government power that threatened their ability to practice their faith in America. James Smart and Michael Whitehead, the attorneys for the victorious students in *Widmar*, were among the first of many public interest lawyers fighting in the courts for religious liberty as well as the sanctity of life and traditional marriage.

The Need for Conservative Religious Liberty Legal Efforts

The First Amendment protects the free exercise of religion, which includes the liberty to publicly acknowledge and worship God. This liberty originates in the higher law, or "the law of nature and of nature's God," as written in the Declaration of Independence. For over 150 years, this religious liberty remained fairly safe in America. While no one would claim that everyone in America was religious, there was a general legal and cultural understanding that religious faith was something to be encouraged and affirmed, and that government could constitutionally acknowledge God's rule in the affairs of men and their governments.[2]

That changed with the 1947 U.S. Supreme Court decision in *Everson v. Board of Education*, in which the words "separation of church and state" (which are found nowhere in the U.S. Constitution) found their way into the majority opinion by liberal Justice Hugo Black, to be misconstrued henceforth to deny religious liberty. Groups such as the American Civil Liberties Union (ACLU) seized the opportunity to initiate a systematic campaign of litigation, disinformation, and intimidation to silence people of faith and stop government acknowledgment of religion with their extreme interpretation of the Establishment Clause.

For decades, these organizations rolled along largely unopposed because those who believed in a balanced, historical understanding of the First Amendment were indifferent, woefully underfunded, poorly trained, or simply unrepresented. Throughout the 1950s and 1960s, through the school prayer cases and others, extremist groups wielded the Establishment Clause as a weapon to obliterate governmental references to religion and the Christian faith and to marginalize people of faith who spoke in the public square about public policy and law from an informed religious perspective.

It seemed as though little could be done as one freedom after another was lost by judicial distortions of the Constitution. Even within the Christian community, many opposed activism in the courts because they viewed it as "worldly" for Christians to fight legal battles and be distracted from pursuing "spiritual" activities.

In the 1970s and 1980s, a new breed of religious liberty lawyers emerged for several reasons. One catalyst was the incessant march of the harsh "separation of church and state" decisions by the courts. Another was the Supreme Court's infamous 1973 *Roe v. Wade* decision, which found a previously overlooked "right to abortion" in the Constitution. *Roe* motivated many to action who believed in the sanctity of life.

Another catalyst was the growing movement to legalize pornography and homosexual and other sexual behavior that most Americans found immoral or contrary to their faith and beliefs. Additionally, many traditional Christians increasingly found themselves the targets of attack, ridicule, or contempt as the representatives of an old, "repressive" America that the secular activists wanted to oust. Those who believed in traditional values realized it was time to act.

The Genesis of Religious Liberty Legal Groups

It is hard to pinpoint exactly when the freedom-based legal groups for religious liberties began. One of the first major signs of life came from the persevering legal work of William Bentley Ball of Harrisburg, Pennsylvania. In the 1970s, in *Lemon v. Kurtzman* and other cases, Ball argued valiantly at the Supreme Court for an end to extreme, modernist interpretations of the Establishment Clause. He won a major free exercise case in *Wisconsin v. Yoder* in 1972 when the Supreme Court upheld the right of an Amish family to opt out of a Wisconsin law requiring them to send their children to public schools that were in conflict with their religious beliefs. William Ball remained active in many cases at the Supreme Court during the 1980s and 1990s, including a significant victory in the 1993 *Zobrest v. Catalina Foothills School District* case, which paved the way for many of the later successful school choice cases, such as the Cleveland school voucher case in 2002.

Another early sign of legal activism for religious liberty was the work of the Christian Law Association, formed by David C. Gibbs, Jr., of the Gibbs and Craze law firm in Cleveland. Beginning in the 1970s, the Christian Law Association fought in court for private evangelical Christian schools and churches suffering persecution from intrusive governmental regulation. The group continues its work today from Seminole, Florida.

However, the beginning of the modern religious liberty public interest movement seems best placed in the early 1980s, when a cluster of events heralded the significant shift by conservative Christians to legal activism. The first event was the huge victory in 1981 at the Supreme Court in *Widmar v. Vincent*. It was one of the first cases in which the Christian community went on the offense against a governmental entity in federal court, asserting a creative and ambitious equal access theory for the freedom of speech rights of religious speakers in government forums. Many had not predicted the huge, emphatic stamp of approval that the Supreme Court gave to their innovative legal theory of equal access. This was the first big court win of the new religious liberty movement.

In immediate response to the *Widmar* decision, the Center for Law and Religious Freedom—founded by the Christian Legal

Society in 1975 to fight for equal access—opened a two-front battle in Congress and the courts to extend *Widmar*'s protection to high school student Bible groups. Many public high schools around the country were denying these groups the right to meet for prayer and Bible study.

On the court front, center attorneys sought Supreme Court review of a high school equal access case in Lubbock, Texas. The Lubbock Civil Liberties Union had won a federal appellate decision requiring the school district to ban student religious groups in its high school. While the Supreme Court denied review, the 23 U.S. senators who joined the center's *amicus* brief became the nucleus of support for equal access legislation in Congress.

Center attorneys drafted the Equal Access Act, which was introduced by Senator Mark Hartfield (R–OR) on September 17, 1982. In 1984, the act passed the Senate by a vote of 88 to 11 and the House by a vote of 337 to 77. It was signed into law by President Reagan on August 11, 1984.

Although the final margin of victory was overwhelming, the battle was exceedingly close as liberal groups fiercely lobbied against passage. Dr. James Dobson of Focus on the Family played a critical role when his many radio listeners inundated congressional offices with calls in favor of the act—until congressional aides begged for the calls to stop.

At the same time, the Center for Law and Religious Freedom pressed ahead in the courts and took the first high school equal access case to the Supreme Court in 1985 on behalf of Williamsport, Pennsylvania, students. Jim Smart argued *Bender v. City of Williamsport*, but the Court dodged a ruling on the merits. Four justices, however, wrote strong opinions in favor of the students' right to equal access. Their reasoning became the basis of the 1990 *Mergens* decision that eventually upheld the constitutionality of the Equal Access Act.

In addition, on the heels of the *Widmar* victory, several litigation groups sprang up. John Whitehead (no relation to Michael

Whitehead of *Widmar* fame) started the Rutherford Institute in 1982 to defend the rights of people of faith. This was a natural outgrowth of Whitehead's book, *The Second American Revolution*, which called on Christians to leave apathy for activism in reaction to the growing secularization of America. Many of the attorneys active in the early days of the religious liberty public interest law movement were inspired to action by this book.

Another major sign of activism occurred in 1983 when Michael Farris moved from Washington state to Washington, D.C., to start two legal operations: the litigation arm of Beverly LaHaye's Concerned Women for America and the Home School Legal Defense Association, a membership of home-schooling families working together to protect their method of educating their children. Both organizations would win significant court victories in the years to come. Farris, for example, won a unanimous victory for CWA at the Supreme Court in the 1986 *Witters* case. Justice Thurgood Marshall wrote for a unanimous Court that the Establishment Clause did not justify a Washington state law singling out theology as the only major for which blind people could not study if they received funding from a special educational aid program for disabled persons.

The Reagan administration helped fuel the growing number of pro-freedom public interest legal groups. President Reagan's leadership in the White House sparked optimism that traditionalists had not felt in years. Also, as more and more of Reagan's judicial appointees assumed seats on the federal bench, conservative public interest lawyers found jurists with minds open to many of their arguments.

As the 1980s wore on, many other groups—such as the National Legal Foundation; the Children's Legal Foundation, an anti-pornography group first founded in the 1970s; Free Speech Advocates; the Western Center for Law and Religious Freedom; Liberty Counsel in Orlando, Florida; and Christian Advocates

Serving Evangelism—either came forward to litigate cases or added litigation to their existing efforts. Two other key individuals, David Langdon and Nate Kellum, would become involved a few years later. Pro-freedom lawyers saw that they could win in court just as their ideological opponents in the ACLU and other liberal activist groups did.

It is important to note that most of these new groups tackled more than just religious liberty issues. They viewed their purpose as to preserve a traditional American legal worldview rooted in Judeo–Christian principles. That meant that they opposed the judicial activism of liberal courts that altered the Constitution in order to advance liberal political goals. They opposed *Roe v. Wade*'s right to abortion, extreme separationist interpretations of the Establishment Clause, and the growing threat to constitutional rights presented by the homosexual activists. Not all groups involved in religious liberty issues were new. Mountain States Legal Foundation became involved in preventing the establishment of religion on federal lands when those lands were closed to the public because they were "sacred" to some American Indians.

The groups also supported broad application of First Amendment rights to freedom of speech and press (but strongly opposed pornography), free exercise of religion, and freedom of conscience and association. They also supported constitutional protection for parents to raise their children without undue interference from the state. The federal courts, even the Supreme Court, began to see their *amicus* briefs in a wide array of constitutional cases.

Public School Curriculum Battles of the 1980s

Despite these positive factors, the freedom-based religious liberty groups did not have major success in one substantial area: litigating for religious liberty and parental rights with regard to the public school curriculum. In other words, the right of parents to have their children opt out of classroom materials that they viewed as objectionable or that they felt violated their personal religious beliefs.

During the 1980s, to many Americans, these public school curriculum cases became the public face of the conservative religious liberty activists.

Michael Farris of Concerned Women for America litigated the "Tennessee Textbook" (*Mozert v. Hawkins County Board of Education*) case against an eastern Tennessee school district that refused to allow students to choose an alternative reading series instead of one chosen by the school district that was filled with politically correct notions favoring animal rights, occultism, environmentalism, and a theological syncretism opposed to Christian beliefs upholding Jesus Christ's unique role in the redemption of mankind. The families argued that the Free Exercise Clause and parental rights gave them the constitutional right to opt out of reading the materials they found offensive.

People for the American Way jumped into the case in a major way, hiring the prestigious Washington, D.C., firm of Wilmer, Cutler and Pickering to represent the school district against the "fundamentalist" insurgents. The eight-day trial in the summer of 1986 attracted media attention from around the world. Later that fall, the federal judge ruled in favor of the Christian parents, shocking the educational establishment and landing their victory on the front page of *The Washington Post* and other newspapers.

Around the same time, another case challenged aspects of the public school curriculum in Alabama as promoting the religion of secular humanism in violation of the Establishment Clause. In 1986, the federal judge hearing the case agreed with the Alabama parents. Although they won at the district court levels in both Tennessee and Alabama, the Christian parents lost at their respective federal appeals courts and were denied review by the Supreme Court.

The only public school curriculum case to reach the Supreme Court was the Louisiana creationism case, *Edwards v. Aguillard* (1987), argued by Wendell Bird. In this case, the Supreme Court, in a 7 to 2 opinion written by Justice William Brennan, ruled against the state of Louisiana's "Balanced Treatment Act," which required that schools teach both creationism and evolution.

As a result, most conservative groups now give litigating public school curriculum cases a much lower priority than they did in the 1980s and have redirected their energies to parental choice in education and other issues.

The Emerging Home Schooling Movement

One of the great successes of the freedom-based religious liberty legal organizations was the legal effort to establish the right of parents to home school their children. The charge was led by the Home School Legal Defense Association. Its founder, Michael Farris, and attorneys Michael Smith and Chris Klicka masterminded an effective legal strategy that took home schooling from a criminal offense in many states to legal status in all 50 states in the span of less than 15 years. Home-schooling families joined the group for an annual membership of $100 and in return received free legal representation if the authorities threatened their home schooling.

Association attorneys fought major cases in Texas, Michigan, North Dakota, and elsewhere, challenging such restrictions on home schooling as laws requiring that all children be taught by state-certified teachers, laws that gave unbridled discretion to school officials to approve or disapprove requests to home school, and policies that insisted on intrusive "home visits" during which school officials demanded to interview home-schooled children without their parents being present. The association, through litigation and lobbying at the state legislatures, abolished these obstacles to home schooling in an outstanding display of collective action by like-minded citizens who were determined to ensure that the government honored their liberties.

The Supreme Court Limits Protection for Religious Freedom

The Supreme Court surprised many on both the Right and the Left with its unexpected decision limiting the protective reach of the Free Exercise Clause in *Employment Division of Oregon v. Smith* (1990). Although some legal commentators on the Right applauded the decision, many attorneys in the conservative religious liberty movement condemned the decision as an erroneous and unwarranted judicial limitation on the free exercise of religion.

In *Employment Division v. Smith*, two drug and alcohol abuse rehabilitation counselors were fired after they ingested peyote, a hallucinogenic drug, during a religious ceremony at an American Indian church. The two men then filed for unemployment benefits with the Oregon Employment Division, and the state denied their request even though the use of peyote was part of their religious practice and supposedly protected by the First Amendment. Most expected the Indians to lose on the grounds that the government has a compelling governmental interest in stopping illegal drug use. Instead, the Supreme Court ruled that the government could forbid any religious practice as long as it did so with a law that was, on its face, neutral toward religion and generally applicable to all.

This profoundly weakened First Amendment protections for religious liberty. Churches and religious organizations faced numerous legal challenges from local and state governments that sought to restrict their free exercise of religion.

Groups from across the political spectrum, alarmed at this severe limitation on religious liberty, worked together to pass the Religious Freedom Restoration Act in 1993. This legislation prohibited the government from limiting a person's free exercise of religion—unless the government had a compelling interest in doing so. In 1997, however, the Supreme Court declared the act unconstitutional as applied to the states in *City of Boerne v. Flores*.

In *Boerne v. Flores*, the local Catholic archbishop had applied for a building permit to enlarge a church in Boerne, Texas. The city denied the permit because the church was located in a "historical district," and the church challenged the restrictions placed on renovating the church building, stating that the city had violated its rights under the Religious Freedom Restoration Act. The Supreme Court struck down the act as exceeding Congress's authority under the Fourteenth Amendment. After the Supreme Court struck down the act, Congress enacted a more targeted protection for religious liberty in the Religious Land Use and Institutionalized Persons Act, which is currently being challenged in the courts.

Equal Access for Churches and Student-Led Bible Clubs

The fight for equal access began in the 1981 *Widmar* case and continues to this day, with major victories along the way. In 1990, the Supreme Court gave a major boost to the ability of student-led religious groups to meet in public schools when it upheld the federal Equal Access Act in *Board of Education v. Mergens*, argued by Jay Sekulow. In *Mergens*, a Nebraska school district had denied the request of a group of Christian students to form an after-school Christian club at their high school. The school district said they could not do so because the meeting was religious. The students filed suit, arguing that the school district's denial violated the 1984 Equal Access Act.

In an 8 to 1 decision, the Supreme Court agreed that students have the right to establish religious clubs in public schools. Today, many public schools allow student Bible clubs, which improve the quality of life at public schools by providing spiritual stability and support for students who desire it.

Mergens also focused the national limelight on an up-and-coming constitutional litigator, Jay Sekulow of Atlanta. Jay had won an earlier Supreme Court decision striking down restrictions on leafleting at the Los Angeles Airport. Pat Robertson of the Christian Broadcasting Network asked Jay in 1990 to assist in developing the American Center for Law and Justice. Jay Sekulow became one of the leading First Amendment lawyers to argue before the Supreme Court, nearly a dozen times before the high court by the end of 2003.

Many of the lawyers who work for the center or who have worked there in the past have become the workhorses of current religious liberty litigation. Ben Bull, Walter Weber, Vincent McCarthy, Jim Henderson, Gary McCaleb, Stuart Roth, Kevin Theriot, the late Mark Troobnick, and others have litigated many of the religious liberty cases argued for the past 15 years or so.

Three years after the start of the American Center for Law and Justice, in 1993, Jay Sekulow and Jordan Lorence won another equal access case at the Supreme Court. They represented a local church called Lamb's Chapel, which had requested to rent a school building to show a Focus on the Family film series that addressed parenting issues from a religious perspective. The Long Island school district denied their request to meet because the film series was religious. Sekulow won a unanimous Supreme Court decision striking down the school district's anti-religious speech policy as unconstitutional viewpoint discrimination.

In 2001, the Supreme Court once again ruled in favor of equal access in *Good News Club v. Milford Central School*, rebuking the federal appeals court for New York, the Second Circuit, for its continuing resistance to the First Amendment's equal access principles. Two years later, in 2003, the Second Circuit reversed 15 years of defiant decisions by submitting to equal access in *Bronx Household of Faith v. Board of Education*, funded and litigated by the Alliance Defense Fund.

Advancing Effectiveness: The Alliance Defense Fund

The effectiveness of the religious liberty groups increased significantly with creation of the Alliance Defense Fund. By the early 1990s, it was obvious that religious liberty could be advanced more effectively if the pro-freedom public interest law movement overcame the lack of funding for cases, the lack of strategic coordination of litigation efforts among the existing organizations, and the lack of training to increase the ranks of effective litigators.

To remedy these problems, over 30 religious leaders met in 1993 through a conference call. They were a who's who of the evangelical community, such as the late Dr. Bill Bright of Campus Crusade for Christ, the late Larry Burkett of Crown Financial Ministries, Dr. James Dobson of Focus on the Family, Dr. D. James Kennedy of Coral Ridge Ministries, the late Marlin Maddoux of the *Point of View* radio program, and others. The result of the conference call was the creation of the Alliance Defense Fund with Alan E. Sears as its president and CEO. The fund opened its doors in January 1994.

Its mission was to provide the training, coordination, and funding for all of the religious liberty legal groups so that no case would be lost because of insufficient resources or lack of experience. The fund would focus its funding, training, and strategy on the legal areas of religious liberty and the sanctity of life and traditional values, including the defense of marriage. Many existing groups and individual attorneys joined the alliance. Strategies were decided by consensus.

Approximately a year after the Alliance Defense Fund opened its doors, the wisdom of having such an organization became clear. It helped win two crucial cases at the Supreme Court in the spring of 1995: the Boston St. Patrick's Day parade case (*Hurley v. Irish-American Gay, Lesbian, and Bisexual Group of Boston*) and *Rosenberger v. Rector*, involving a discriminatory funding system at the University of Virginia that excluded only student Christian publications from funding.

The *Hurley* case reached the Supreme Court because of the courage of one attorney: Chester Darling, who represented the veterans group that sponsored the annual Boston St. Patrick's

Day parade. The veterans declined to allow a homosexual group to march in the parade, and the group sued the veterans under the Massachusetts antidiscrimination law. Homosexual activists pummeled the veterans at every level of the liberal Massachusetts court system. Darling convinced the dispirited veterans group to appeal the case to the U.S. Supreme Court and cashed in his last retirement account to pay for the printing of the documents. The Supreme Court took the case.

Alliance entered the case, supplying major funding to Chester Darling and the veterans for the appeal and relieving them of the distracting search for money. It had experienced attorneys help Darling prepare his brief. Former Attorney General Edwin Meese III and The Heritage Foundation organized a moot court where experienced Supreme Court lawyers prepared Darling for the fast and furious questioning typical of a Supreme Court case. The moot courts at Heritage have now become an important vehicle to prepare conservative lawyers for important cases at the Supreme Court.

Darling won a unanimous victory at the Supreme Court in June 1995. The Court ruled that the discrimination lawsuit violated the veterans' freedom "not to speak" by forcing them to present a message that they opposed. This victory helped lead to the 2000 decision in *Boy Scouts of America v. Dale*. That case recognized the First Amendment rights of a private organization to exclude from leadership those whose behavior contradicts the message espoused by the organization. The Alliance Defense Fund coordinated and funded many of the *amicus* briefs filed in *Boy Scouts*, and the attorney for the Scouts participated in a moot court sponsored by The Heritage Foundation. The successful outcome demonstrated yet again the importance of working together to advance First Amendment freedoms.

The ADF also aided the attorneys handling the *Rosenberger* case before the Supreme Court. In that case, the University of Virginia, while funding all other student publications, refused to fund an evangelical Christian student newspaper on campus because it was religious. The Center for Individual Rights, based in Washington, D.C., doggedly represented the Christian students. It funded the appeal to the Supreme Court, and its lawyers participated in moot courts to prepare Michael McConnell, who argued the case for the students and now sits as a federal appeals court judge in Utah. In June 1995, the Supreme Court ruled 5 to 4 that the University of Virginia acted unconstitutionally by singling out student religious publications for exclusion from funding.

And the win in *Rosenberger* keeps on making a difference. The Supreme Court has cited it in such equal access wins as the *Good News Club* case in 2001. Justice Clarence Thomas, in the *Good News Club* opinion, mentions ADF-funded cases that created a split in the circuit courts as the reason for granting review of the case. The Supreme Court cited *Rosenberger*'s equal access principles in upholding the Cleveland school voucher program in 2002 and in other cases involving government funding of education programs at private religious schools, such as *Mitchell v. Helms.*

In contrast to the ADF's well-coordinated, well-financed assistance to Supreme Court advocates, consider the solitary efforts of James Smart in *Widmar* in 1981. Smart had no money except for a few hundred dollars donated by the student group at the University of Missouri. He had no access to experienced Supreme Court advocates to help him prepare for his oral arguments. He could not afford to coordinate *amicus* briefs to support him. Although Smart won because of his valiant and sacrificial efforts, ADF has provided millions of dollars of support for litigation and exists to make sure that important cases do not have to labor under so many impediments to victory.

The Alliance Defense Fund has expanded its services by funding training programs for attorneys—completed by more than

700 individuals—and a separate training program for law students in order to expand the current force of religious liberty attorneys and build for the future. It also has sought a consensus among its allies to determine the litigation priorities for the near future. These priorities include:

- **Defending** marriage by fighting same-sex marriage cases and domestic partnerships cases determined by the judicial activism of unelected judges. Our nation cannot long survive if the unelected courts can change the basic foundation of our society—marriage consisting of one man and one woman to raise and nurture children.

- **Convincing** the Supreme Court to rein in its judicial activism by reversing *Roe v. Wade* (where it discovered a right to abortion); *Lemon v. Kurtzman* (the Supreme Court's much maligned and erroneous Establishment Clause test); and *Lawrence v. Texas* (discovering a dubious "right to sodomy" in the Constitution). Our constitutional republic can sustain itself only if judges maintain their proper role in a federalist system of separation of powers and defer to the public policy decisions of the people and their elected representatives.

- **Confirming** the constitutional power of government to acknowledge our nation's Judeo–Christian heritage by posting the Ten Commandments in public buildings and saying "under God" in the Pledge of Allegiance and elsewhere.

- **Protecting** the freedom of conscience and association of those threatened by zealous, politically correct prosecutions under nondiscrimination laws. Some officials are now requiring religious organizations renting spaces at public universities and public schools to promise that they will not require their members or officers to adhere to their religious beliefs. How can a Buddhist or an atheist lead a campus Bible study or a Jewish group?

- **Allowing** business owners—such as a Catholic printer in Vermont who refuses to print pro-abortion material or an evangelical woman who owns a bridal gown store and declines to sell dresses to two women who want to use them in a same-sex "commitment" ceremony—to refuse work on the basis of conscience. Some officials apply "hate crime" laws against those who believe homosexuals can change or to silence other statements deemed "offensive" by the dominant worldview of our increasingly secularized society. A free society cannot tolerate such authoritarian repression of individual liberty.

- **Protecting** churches from restrictive and unconstitutional zoning ordinances. In many communities, zoning plans do not give houses of worship any place to locate as a matter of right. They must seek the government's permission to meet or build anywhere in the city or county. Ironically, the Supreme Court has ruled that it is unconstitutional for a city to zone out pornography theaters in the same way. Therefore, the ADF and its allies have been arguing that the courts "please recognize the same constitutional rights for churches that pornography theaters already have."

- **Fighting** the insidious trend at the Supreme Court of referring to international law to understand the protections granted us by the Constitution. The Supreme Court evinces a growing fascination with international law as long as it comes from liberal, secular Western Europe. Seemingly, our nation has come full circle and is returning to a legal system that our Founding Fathers rejected—a system based on the law of man rather than on the "laws of nature and of nature's God" as set forth in the Declaration of Independence.

It will be the religious liberty law movement's role to remain actively engaged in our nation's judicial system to protect and defend our religious freedom. The tremendous strides in training, coordinating, and funding over the past decade have strengthened the movement and prepared it to take on the many legal challenges ahead. The challenges are large, and daunting on the surface, but because of the tremendous sacrifice and service by all those who have fought so hard to preserve religious liberty, this is a battle that can be won. The Alliance Defense Fund and its allies are dedicated to such a victory.

---

[1] My thanks to Craig Osten and Jordan Lorence for their help in writing this chapter.

[2] Joseph Story, who was appointed to the Supreme Court by President James Madison and became one of its most respected justices, wrote in his *Commentaries on the Constitution of the United States* in 1833: "Probably at the time of the adoption of the constitution, and of the amendment to it ... sentiment in America, was that Christianity ought to receive encouragement from the state, so far as was not incompatible with the private rights of conscience, and the freedom of religious worship."

CHAPTER 5

Economic Liberty and Judicial Activism

William H. Mellor

Every day, hundreds of thousands of Americans engage in massive expressions of civil disobedience. They face arrest, fines, and even imprisonment as a result of their actions. You won't find these people on picket lines or being hauled away in paddy wagons after raucous demonstrations. They all seek the same goal: to earn an honest living for themselves and their families. Tragically, they do so under the laws and regulations of cities and states across the nation that make them outlaws.

That these hard-working men and women should be treated as pariahs under the laws of this land is the legacy of the Supreme Court's 1872 decision in the *Slaughter-House Cases*[1] and its total evisceration of constitutional protection for economic liberty.

The *Slaughter-House Cases*, in a sharply divided 5 to 4 decision, allowed the bribe-induced Louisiana Legislature to create a 25-year monopoly for slaughtering livestock. The legislature granted one company the exclusive authority to operate a slaughterhouse in New Orleans and required all other butchers to use that facility and to pay for its services. Butchers who lost their livelihoods challenged the law as a violation of the recently enacted Fourteenth Amendment, which stated that "No state shall make or enforce any law which shall abridge the privileges or immunities of citizens of the United States." Since the legislative history of the amendment contained various references to protecting contracts, property, and livelihoods, it seemed clear that economic liberty was to be a privilege of citizenship protected from state infringement by this new constitutional provision.

Unfortunately for the butchers then and for other Americans today, the Court disagreed. Ignoring original intent, the majority held that "privileges or immunities" encompassed only a very limited number of rights expressly recognized by the original Constitution, such as access to foreign commerce and navigable waters, habeas corpus, and freedom of movement from state to state. But it did not include the Bill of Rights or economic liberty. Without unambiguous constitutional protection, economic liberty was buffeted by ever-encroaching government restrictions over the ensuing decades.

The final blow occurred in *United States v. Carolene Products*,[2] in which, through a mere footnote, the Supreme Court relegated economic liberty to second-class status under the Constitution. With such diminished stature, economic liberty became subject to sweeping legislative control beyond judicial scrutiny. Rapid growth of economic regulations at the federal, state, and local levels accelerated virtually unchecked.

What sorts of people persevere in the face of such legal adversity? They are people like Hector Ricketts, who immigrated to America 25 years ago to start a new life as a hospital worker. When he lost his job, he could have gone on welfare or drawn unemployment. Instead, he decided to go into the commuter van business providing safe, efficient, low-cost transportation throughout his community in Queens, New York. Every day, Hector transported several thousand people to and from work and around his neighborhood, and he was not alone. Hundreds of other enterprising van operators transported nearly 40,000 people daily throughout Queens and Brooklyn. Hector had a loyal clientele and an unblemished safety record. He put people to work and took people to work.

You would think that in a city where over 10 percent of the population is on public assistance and nearly 20 percent of the economy operates in the black market, such honest enterprise would be encouraged. You would be wrong. Under the laws of New York, it was illegal for Hector Ricketts and his colleagues to operate because they competed with bus monopolies created by the city. The city council effectively rigged the system by requiring a permit but then establishing procedures that made it impossible to obtain one. Vans were regularly confiscated, and operators were forced to pay onerous fines.

An Iron Triangle

Meanwhile, on the same routes that vans served for a dollar a ride, the bus monopolies provided dismal service subsidized up to $3.95 per rider in addition to a $1.50 fare. An iron triangle of the city council, the Transit Workers Union, and the bus company foreclosed avenues of competition or legal redress. This capture of the regulatory and legislative process, so clearly predicted by public choice theory, is the ubiquitous legacy of the *Slaughter-House Cases* and the resulting judicial deference to legislative prerogative in economic matters.

Then there are people like Taalib-din Uqdah and his wife Pamela Ferrell, who in the early 1980s opened up the first African hair-braiding salon in the District of Columbia. Taking the $500 that they had received for selling their car, they launched their enterprise with a lot of energy, unbridled hope, and a vision of hair braiding as both a business and a cultural art form. Before long, they were thriving, employing 10 people in their salon.

Then one day came the knock on the door. Upon opening the door, Taalib-din was faced with the cosmetology police who demanded to see his license. Taalib-din informed the man that he had no license but that he would obtain one, assuming that this would be a modest inconvenience at most.

Imagine his surprise when he learned that, in order to braid hair in the District of Columbia, you needed a cosmetology license that required in turn 1,500 hours of class work over a period of some six to nine months at a cost of $5,000. As is often the case with licensing regimes, these requirements were imposed by a board composed of individuals licensed in the field they were regulating—i.e., cosmetologists. Virtually the entire 1,500 hours was spent on subjects irrelevant to natural hair care and hair braiding. At the end of such training, he would have to demonstrate his proficiency in finger waves and pin curls, hairstyles popular on white women in 1938 when the law was passed. And if that wasn't bad enough, in order to run the salon, he would need a manager's license that required further training.

Taalib-din, like Hector and so many other entry-level entrepreneurs faced with similar unreasonable requirements, made the very rational decision to continue doing business and ignore the licensing requirements. This, of course, doomed any effort to increase business, obtain financing through normal channels, or even to advertise. Nevertheless, the business continued to provide a good living for Taalib-din, Pamela, and their employees. Before long, there was another knock on the door. Taalib-din was informed that operating without a license exposed him to a fine of up to $1,000 per day plus time in jail.

Both Hector and Taalib-din went to court, represented by the Institute for Justice. Hector succeeded in having his van business deregulated significantly and gained widespread recognition after September 11 when he organized van operators to provide free transportation for thousands of rescue workers and victims' families. Taalib-din and Pamela have a thriving business in the District of Columbia in the aftermath of deregulation made possible through their courageous efforts and, in classic entrepreneurial fashion, have gone on to be advocates for natural hair care and braiding across the country, trying to remove barriers like the ones they confronted that still exist in many states in the nation.

Stifling Free Enterprise

These are but two of the countless heroes who struggle daily against arbitrary and irrational laws used by state and local governments to condition entry into markets. While there has been no comprehensive documentation of all licensing laws that exist at the state and local levels, knowledgeable experts think that at least 10 percent of the occupations in this country have licenses attached as a condition to entry.

The onus of these laws falls most heavily on people like Hector and Taalib-din who have little in the way of capital or formal education and for whom these barriers do not merely mean inconvenience or an incremental increase in the cost of doing business, but rather make the difference between entering the formal economy and being doomed to live as economic outsiders or welfare recipients.

The problem is that, in the aftermath of the *Slaughter-House Cases*, courts routinely defer to such monopolies and licensing regimes. The standard for judicial review is so lenient that, for all practical purposes, there doesn't even need to be a fit between any asserted public health and safety goals and the means chosen by government to reach these goals.

Indeed, any reasonably *conceivable* facts that might justify a law can be the basis for upholding economic regulations law even if such facts were never contemplated by the legislature when it passed the law. Not only that, but the actual existence of any such facts justifying the law need not actually be demonstrated by the state when the law is challenged. This means that today, even in the aftermath of welfare reform, the right to earn an honest living receives less legal protection than the "right" to a welfare check.

In the absence of the Privileges and Immunities Clause, courts have drawn on other constitutional provisions and developed a variety of legal theories to constrain economic regulation, the most controversial being substantive due process. Ultimately, these alternative constitutional provisions have proved inadequate for a task they were never clearly intended to perform. As long as the *Slaughter-House Cases* remain the law of the land, economic liberty will remain in constitutional exile.

The growth of economic regulation blessed by court edict was dramatically accelerated through determined and creative advocacy by a host of liberal public interest law firms that proliferated in the 1960s and 1970s. Groups like the Natural Resources Defense Council, Public Citizen, and Legal Services Corporation joined old-line groups like the ACLU, NAACP Legal Defense and Education Fund, and Sierra Club to urge a greater role for government in a variety of economic and property matters.

So effective were these groups that in 1971, attorney Lewis Powell, later to be a justice on the Supreme Court, wrote a memo to the U.S. Chamber of Commerce entitled "Attack on America's Free Enterprise System." In his memo, Powell wrote, "The judiciary may be the most important instrument of social, economic, and political change."[3]

THE NATIONAL LEGAL CENTER FOR THE PUBLIC INTEREST

The National Legal Center for the Public Interest was founded in 1975 to create a network of independent public interest law organizations around the country, patterned after the Pacific Legal Foundation in California. The center's first president was Leonard Theberge, who in just three years created 10 legal foundations, including the Mountain States Legal Foundation, the Southeastern Legal Foundation, what is now the Atlantic Legal Foundation, and the Gulf and Great Plains Legal Foundation, which later became the Landmark Legal Foundation. After nearly 30 years, all four of these groups remain active and are among the most successful organizations in the freedom-based public interest law movement.

Having accomplished its mission, the National Legal Center's board had a choice: close down the organization or develop a new mission. The board decided there was important work to be done in the non-litigation field, and after moving to Washington, D.C., it selected businessman Ernest B. Hueter as president, a position he has held for almost 24 years.

The National Legal Center for the Public Interest fosters knowledge of the law and the administration of justice in a society committed to individual rights, free enterprise, private property, limited government, a balanced use of private and public resources, and a fair and efficient judiciary. Its primary audience, explains Hueter, is "the private sector—business, industry, and agriculture."

The center fulfills its mission with a comprehensive educational and information program that includes the publication of a monthly monograph series on business issues that are important to

lawyers in private practice, as well as a monthly legal newsletter. In its publications and events, the center makes it a point to concentrate on the concerns of corporate general counsel and business lawyers, although it also communicates with and uses the services of legal educators, primarily professors of law.

The center's best-known public event is the annual Gauer Distinguished Lecture in Law and Public Policy, always held in New York City. The 2003 lecturer was Condoleezza Rice, national security adviser to President George W. Bush. Past speakers at the black-tie banquet have included Ronald Reagan, George H. W. Bush, Colin Powell, Lady Margaret Thatcher, and Judge William H. Webster.

Other popular center programs are "A Day With Justice," during which senior Justice Department officials brief attendees, and "The Supreme Court Press Briefing," held for legal journalists just prior to the Court's new term. The center also sponsors the "General Counsel Briefing" for corporate counsel and business attorneys in private practice as well as a legal intern program for students interested in government.

First as the creator of some 10 litigating foundations and now as a leading participant in the ongoing debate about a free and just society, the National Legal Center for the Public Interest has played a major role in the development of the freedom-based public interest law movement.

Lee Edwards

Reasons for Hope

Bleak though the current state of affairs may be, and however long the intervening years, four trends offer hope for the prospect of eventually overturning the *Slaughter-House Cases* and restoring constitutional vitality to the Privileges and Immunities Clause.

First, the maturing of the freedom-based public interest law movement, first launched in the 1970s, has put advocates for economic liberty in courtrooms across America. The Pacific Legal Foundation, Washington Legal Foundation, Mountain States Legal Foundation, New England Legal Foundation, Atlantic Legal Foundation, and others have all in various ways pursued cutting-edge litigation seeking to roll back the excesses of economic regulation unleashed by the *Carolene Products* decision.

Typically focused on federal laws and regulations, these organizations have shown how important it is for large bureaucracies to be called to account through litigation. Their track record is impressive, whether in striking down unreasonable environmental regulations or in securing protection for property owners faced with unconstitutional takings. Clearly, the liberal public interest groups, though larger and far better funded, now have adversaries they must reckon with.

Much of the bloom is off the rose of the environmental movement, for example, thanks to high-profile cases taken by the freedom-based public interest law movement. The environmental lobby may have reached its apogee with Al Gore's 1992 book *Earth in the Balance*, in which he asserted "growing evidence of an ecological holocaust" that required a "wrenching transformation of society."[4] Sweeping and vastly expensive laws like Superfund and the Clean Air Act were passed accompanied by similarly apocalyptic rhetoric. Freedom-based public interest law firms have fought effectively to limit excesses of such laws and to educate the general public. Today, as a result, Gore's extreme views are in retreat.

Second, there is the growing body of scholarship that challenges the moral and legal underpinnings of the *Slaughter-House Cases*. Virtually every serious scholar, liberal or conservative, who has examined the case believes that it was wrongly decided. This scholarship and its attendant intellectual ferment offer crucial impetus to reverse this pernicious precedent.[5] Indeed, the Supreme Court offered the enticing prospect of revisiting the Privileges and Immunities Clause by citing it as the basis for recognizing the right to travel in *Saenz v. Roe*,[6] a move that caught many Court watchers by surprise. And the Institute for Justice, pursuing its long-term strategy of overturning the *Slaughter-House Cases*, has secured notable victories for economic liberty in, for example, *Cornwell v. Hamilton*[7] and *Craigmiles v. Giles*.[8]

Coinciding with this ferment is the Supreme Court's apparent willingness over the past decade, in cases like *Lucas v. South Carolina Coastal Council*[9] and *United States v. Lopez*[10] to recognize some outer boundaries on heretofore unchecked government authority. Perhaps most promising, Chief Justice William Rehnquist, in *Dolan v. City of Tigard*,[11] seemed to open the door to eliminating the dichotomy between preferred constitutional rights and those, like economic liberty and property rights, that are accorded inferior treatment. "We see no reason," wrote Rehnquist, "why the takings clause of the Fifth Amendment, as much a part of the Bill of Rights as the First or Fourth Amendment, should be relegated to the status of a poor relation...."

Meanwhile, overwhelming evidence and a mounting consensus recognize the failure of the welfare state, particularly in the inner cities of America. This provides a sociopolitical climate ripe for arguments in favor of opening up entry-level opportunities and removing unnecessary governmental constraints on inner-city enterprise.

To decide what should replace the *Slaughter-House Cases*, there is no better place to start than the dissents of Justices Joseph Bradley, Stephen Field, and Noah Swayne. There you will find a foundation for economic liberty that recognizes, as Justice Bradley said, the right "of every American citizen to adopt and follow lawful industrial pursuit—not injurious to the community—as he may see fit without unreasonable regulation or molestation." Governmental power could still be exercised to protect public health and safety, but not to create monopolies or to impose irrational conditions upon market entry.

The rankest form of judicial activism is that which reads out of the Constitution rights that clearly are protected. The *Slaughter-House Cases* stand as a grim testament to the real world consequences of such irresponsible judicial activism.

For all of these reasons, the *Slaughter-House Cases* and their progeny must be overturned. The sanctity of our Constitution compels it; the accountability of our governing institutions demands it. Admittedly, this is a tough challenge, but in the coming years, we should remember entrepreneurs like Hector and Taalib-din who aspire to nothing more than their share of the American Dream. How can we let illegitimate precedent stand in their way?

---

[1] 83 U.S. (16 Wall.) 36 (1873).

[2] 304 U.S. 144 (1938).

[3] Lewis F. Powell, "The Powell Memorandum: Attack on American Free Enterprise System," August 23, 1971, published and distributed by the U.S. Chamber of Commerce.

[4] Al Gore, *Earth in the Balance: Ecology and the Human Spirit* (Boston, Houghton Mifflin Company, 1992), pp. 245, 274.

[5] See, e.g., Richard L. Aynes, *On Misreading John Bingham and the Fourteenth Amendment*, 103 Yale L.J. 57 (1993); David A. J. Richards, *Conscience and the Constitution: History, Theory, and Law of the Reconstruction Amendments* 204–217 (1993); Akhil Reed Amar, *The Bill of Rights and the Fourteenth Amendment*, 101 Yale L.J. 1193, 1257-59 (1992); Clint Bolick, *Unfinished Business* (1990); William E. Nelson, *The Fourteenth Amendment: From Political Principle to Judicial Doctrine* 156–64 (1988); Walter F. Murphy, *Slaughter-House, Civil Rights, and the Limits on Constitutional Change*, 32 Amer. J. of Juris. 1, 1–8 (1987); John Hart Ely, *Democracy and Distrust: A Theory of Judicial Review* 22-30 (1980); Laurence H. Tribe, *American Constitutional Law* §§ 7–2 to 7–4, at 415–26, and § 11–2, at 567–69 (1st ed. 1978).

[6] 526 U.S.489 (1999).

[7] 80 F.Supp.2d 1101 (S.D. Cal. 1999).

[8] 110 F.Supp.2d 658 (E.D. Tenn. 2000), *aff'd*, 312 F.3d 220 (6th Cir. 2002).

[9] 505 U.S. 1003.

[10] 514 U.S. 549.

[11] 512 U.S. 374.

CHAPTER 6

Equality Under the Law

Roger Clegg

The Equal Protection Clause of the Fourteenth Amendment to the Constitution and other federal and state civil rights laws ban most discrimination on the basis of race, ethnicity, and sex. There is a broad national consensus that such discrimination is wrong, particularly when it is the government that classifies its citizens and treats some better, and others worse, because of one or more of these immutable characteristics.

Nonetheless, many government entities—including many courts—have concluded that the principle of nondiscrimination protects only members of some groups and not others and that discrimination against whites, or men, or even "overrepresented" minority groups is politically correct, perfectly permissible, and, indeed, essential. Discrimination through quotas and other preferences is widespread.

But it is not as widespread as it might be, thanks to the efforts of the freedom-based public interest legal movement. In landmark case after landmark case—*Adarand Constructors, Inc. v. Peña*, for instance, and *Gratz v. Bollinger, Hopwood v. Texas, Shaw v. Reno, Podberesky v. Kirwan*, and on and on—litigating groups like the Pacific Legal Foundation, Center for Individual Rights, Landmark Legal Foundation, Institute for Justice, Southeastern Legal Foundation, Mountain States Legal Foundation, Washington Legal Foundation, and Individual Rights Foundation have played critical roles. Non-litigating organizations like the Center for Equal Opportunity and American Civil Rights Institute have also been indispensable. The cases discussed in this chapter are only a sampling of the groups' efforts in this area.

Why have the efforts of these groups been so critical in this particular arena? One reason is that attacks on "affirmative action" are, inevitably but unfairly, characterized by the media and intelligentsia as reactionary at best, and frequently as racist. The proponents of this sort of discrimination—such as the civil rights establishment and academia—are well-connected, well-funded, and deeply committed. Politicians and, increasingly, large businesses are reluctant to criticize the use of preferences and are even supportive for various reasons (none of them persuasive).

The result: Those challenging or helping to challenge affirmative action risk ostracism and public condemnation; politicians beholden to special interests refuse to act against these programs and frequently try to expand them; the financial resources needed to mount a challenge are hard to find; and the legal establishment (including not only the professoriate, but also large firms and company general counsel, as well as many judges) is unsympathetic or hostile.

Thus, notwithstanding the enormous unpopularity of preferential treatment among the vast majority of Americans, we have seen a failure of the political, economic, and legal marketplaces to end such discrimination. Fortunately, however, the organizations discussed in this chapter have been willing to step into the breach and defend the interests and principles that are enshrined in law, cherished by most Americans, and essential for the survival of our increasingly multiracial, multiethnic nation.

Pacific Legal Foundation

The Pacific Legal Foundation is a legal advocacy institution with clear objectives aimed at preserving human dignity, individual and economic liberty, free enterprise, and private property in America. One of its many legal objectives is to fight in court to uphold the principle of equal treatment of all citizens under the law.

Specifically, the foundation believes that the benefits of government activities, including employment, education, and public contracts, should be available based on individual merit—and *not* on such factors as race, sex, or ethnicity. The following cases illustrate some of its best work in this area.

Monterey Mechanical Co. v. Wilson involved a general contracting firm that bid on a large utilities upgrade construction project for California Polytechnic University. Monterey Mechanical submitted the lowest bid on this project, but it was rejected in favor of another firm because of a racially preferential law. In a unanimous opinion, the Ninth Circuit panel held that the state statute, on its face, violated Monterey Mechanical's equal protection rights. The court invalidated a state statute that applied to a broad array of state contracting entities.

Thus, as a practical matter, this victory eliminated a great deal of state-sponsored discrimination. Moreover, *Monterey Mechanical* established that so-called outreach programs, or "best efforts" requirements, could violate the Equal Protection Clause if the policy favored minority or women contractors or subcontractors to the exclusion of others, even where no contracting quota needed to be met.

Likewise, *Associated General Contractors v. City and County of San Francisco*, decided on March 23, 1987, represented a major victory for the Pacific Legal Foundation over San Francisco's discriminatory selection process regarding public contracting. The Ninth Circuit ruled in favor of PLF's position that the selection process violated both the competitive bidding requirements of the city's charter and the equal protection guarantee of the Constitution. The ruling in *Associated General Contractors* was later relied upon by the Supreme Court in its 1989 landmark decision in *City of Richmond v. J. A. Croson Co.*

The Pacific Legal Foundation's 30-year battle against government-sponsored race and sex discrimination was greatly aided in November 1996 with the passage of California's Proposition 209, the California Civil Rights Initiative, which amended the state constitution to make it illegal for the government to "discriminate against, or grant preferential treatment to, any individual or group on the basis of race, sex, color, ethnicity, or national origin in the operation of public employment, public education, or public contracting."

The day after Proposition 209 was adopted by the voters, a federal lawsuit was filed challenging California's freshly minted prohibition of racial discrimination on the ground that it discriminated on the basis of race! This argument could have been dismissed as laughable had it not been accepted by a federal district court judge. Apparently undeterred by the irony of his ruling, the judge held that California could not guarantee that its citizens would receive the equal protection of the laws without running afoul of the federal Equal Protection Clause.

The same constitutional provision that had long been misinterpreted to allow certain forms of racial discrimination and preferences had now been twisted into a hopeless non sequitur by a ruling that proclaimed some forms of discrimination are *required* by that provision. It fell to the Ninth Circuit to untie the knots, with the help of the Pacific Legal Foundation. Agreeing with the arguments made in the foundation's friend of the court brief, as well as briefs by other organizations discussed in this chapter, the Ninth Circuit upheld Proposition 209 in *Coalition for Economic Equity v. Wilson.*

Notwithstanding Proposition 209's mandate and the Ninth Circuit's ruling in the *Coalition* case, many public entities in California continue to do their best to thwart the letter and spirit of Proposition

209. Worse, California Attorney General Bill Lockyer, though sworn to uphold and defend the constitution and laws of California, has refused to enforce Proposition 209. Accordingly, the Pacific Legal Foundation stepped into the breach to enforce Proposition 209 against those state and local governments that have refused to comply. Indeed, it is no exaggeration to say that the foundation has been the primary enforcer of Proposition 209 since its passage.

While some government entities have changed their ways of doing business, many others either wait to be sued or foolishly try to defend themselves against enforcement actions brought by the foundation under its Proposition 209 enforcement program— Operation End Bias. Some government entities have tried to circumvent Proposition 209 by implementing programs that require contractors to employ a specific percentage of minority- or women-owned subcontractors. Some agencies also require contractors to hire specific percentages of certain racial groups and women in their own companies.

A few officials have labeled their goals as "aspirational" in attempts to give the appearance that their practices do not discriminate. Still others have offered discretionary waivers to give the appearance that their policies are flexible and not mandatory. (In practice, however, waivers are rarely issued.) The foundation has successfully litigated against these types of policies in cases like *Hi-Voltage Wire Works, Inc. v. City of San Jose* (municipal contracting preferences); *Crawford v. Huntington Beach Union High School District* (K–12 school assignment preferences); and *Kidd v. California* (employment preferences).

Center for Individual Rights

The Center for Individual Rights is a nonprofit public interest law firm dedicated to the defense of individual liberties, which have come under increasing assault by federal, state, and local governments through social engineering, extraconstitutional notions of group rights, and the attempted imposition of a politically correct orthodoxy. The center specializes in a handful of litigation areas, with free speech, civil rights, religious liberty, and federalism being the most important.

The center focuses primarily on original litigation, rather than *amicus* briefs, and strives to make the best use of its limited resources by carefully selecting cases with the greatest potential to set important legal precedents protecting individual rights. What follows is a description of the center's most important cases challenging racial and gender preferences. It represented one or more of the parties in each of these cases.

Higher Education Racial Preference Cases. In what came to be the nation's most important challenge to race-based admissions, the center filed lawsuits in the fall of 1997 against the University of Michigan Law School and undergraduate College of Literature, Science, and the Arts. The goal of *Grutter v. Bollinger* and *Gratz v. Bollinger*, respectively, was to eliminate—both at UM and nationwide—the use of two-track race-based admission systems that employ different, lower admissions standards for minority applicants in order to boost minority enrollment. The lawsuits challenged the claim that campus diversity is a compelling state interest that justifies an exception to the Constitution's equal protection guarantee and Title VI's statutory ban on racial discrimination. The center also argued that the admissions systems at UM were not narrowly tailored to achieve the asserted goal of an intellectually diverse student body, but instead were designed and used to achieve racial balancing for its own sake.

After a combination of victories and defeats in the lower courts, *Grutter* and *Gratz* reached the U.S. Supreme Court, which heard oral argument in the two cases in April 2003. On June 23, the Court issued a split decision, striking down the university's 20-point bonus for college applicants while upholding race-based admissions policies at the law school. In the disappointing law-school decision, the Court found campus diversity compelling enough to justify some consideration of race. It did, however, subject racial admissions preferences to new limits of time and scope.

Specifically, the Supreme Court held that race must be used in a "flexible, nonmechanical way" and cannot generally be a "decisive factor" in admissions. Instead, universities must engage "in a highly individualized, holistic review of each applicant's file, giving serious consideration to all the ways an applicant might contribute to a diverse educational environment." In sum, institutions of higher education may no longer treat race as if it "automatically ensured a specific and identifiable contribution to a university's diversity."

The Michigan decisions also require that universities engage in "serious, good faith consideration of workable race-neutral alternatives that will achieve the diversity the university seeks." Noting the "wide variety of alternative approaches" already being used in states like California, Texas, and Florida, the Supreme Court said that universities must "draw on the most promising aspects of these race-neutral alternatives."

Moreover, each school must conduct "periodic reviews to determine whether racial preferences are still necessary" in order to "terminate its race-conscious admissions program as soon as practicable." In addition, the justices called for "sunset provisions in race-conscious admissions policies" and expressed, at the very least, an expectation that such policies will end within 25 years.

In its landmark 1996 decision in *Hopwood v. Texas*, the U.S. Court of Appeals for the Fifth Circuit struck down the University of Texas School of Law's race-based admissions policies, holding that a desire for student body diversity could not justify the use of race in admissions. The Supreme Court subsequently denied the state's petition for review. The Fifth Circuit ruled that Justice Lewis Powell's 1978 opinion endorsing the diversity rationale—in *Regents v. Bakke*—was not binding Supreme Court precedent.

That ruling sent shock waves throughout the higher education establishment, which had been arguing for two decades that it could rely on Powell's opinion. *Hopwood* remained the most important post-*Bakke* ruling on race-based admissions until it was overruled by the Supreme Court's decision in *Grutter v. Bollinger*.

The Center for Individual Rights represented black students at Alabama State University in a lawsuit challenging white-only "diversity scholarships" at this historically black university. The plaintiffs' separate action was dismissed with leave to intervene in the ongoing desegregation litigation, *Knight v. Alabama*, that had produced the diversity scholarships. After intervening in *Knight*, the plaintiffs succeeded in getting the university to drop the white-only restriction on its diversity scholarships.

Other Preference Litigation. In August 2002, the center filed a lawsuit challenging preferential hiring and promotion goals for women and minorities at the U.S. Department of Housing and Urban Development. The lawsuit charges HUD and the Equal Employment Opportunity Commission—which encourages and approves affirmative action plans at HUD and other agencies—with intentional race and sex discrimination in violation of Title VII and the Constitution's equal protection guarantee.

In *Lamprecht v. Federal Communications Commission*, the center successfully challenged a Federal Communications Commission program aimed at increasing "broadcast diversity," under which female applicants for radio broadcast licenses received a "gender credit" that gave them an advantage over competing male applicants. In a 1992 opinion by Clarence Thomas, who heard the case when he was a D.C. circuit court judge, the court of appeals ruled that the FCC's gender preference program violated the equal protection component of the Fifth Amendment. The D.C. Circuit thus became the first court to rule a federal affirmative action program unconstitutional.

In a suit on behalf of the Bossier Parish, Louisiana, school board, the center sought to curb the U.S. Justice Department's use

of the 1965 Voting Rights Act's pre-clearance provision (Section 5) to force state and local governments to gerrymander voting districts in a way that maximized the number of "minority" districts. On the case's second trip to the Supreme Court, the justices ruled for Bossier Parish in January 2000.

Landmark Legal Foundation and Institute for Justice

In 1988, Clint Bolick launched a D.C.-based Landmark Legal Foundation project called the Center for Civil Rights. That same year, he authored *Changing Course: Civil Rights at the Crossroads*,[1] which set forth an alternative civil rights strategy that coupled opposition to racial preferences with support for individual empowerment. The latter part of the agenda focused on removing barriers to entrepreneurship and advancing school choice, which Bolick has litigated aggressively over the years.

The Center for Civil Rights was aimed at implementing the agenda outlined in *Changing Course*. A key strategy advanced by Bolick to achieve this goal was to transform the terms of the debate by representing minorities who were victims of racial classifications.

In the late 1980s, Landmark Legal Foundation filed a lawsuit on behalf of a California woman, Mary Amaya, and her son, Demond Crawford, challenging the state's ban on the use of I.Q. tests for black youngsters. Amaya wanted to use the test for diagnostic purposes, but the state singled out blacks for exclusion, ostensibly for their benefit. The school district urged Amaya to change Demond's ethnic category to Hispanic because he was half-black and half-Hispanic. She refused, and the lawsuit followed. It helped to underscore the fact that supposedly benevolent racial classifications often hurt the very people they are supposed to benefit. In 1995, a federal judge tossed out California's discriminatory race-based testing restrictions.

Landmark also led the fight to remove racial quotas from the Kansas City, Missouri, desegregation plan. The foundation's

efforts opened the door to thousands of black schoolchildren ironically locked out of the district's new magnet schools by a rigid and arbitrary admissions quota scheme.

In 1991, Bolick joined with William "Chip" Mellor to establish the Institute for Justice. In the mid-1990s, the institute took on the issue of barriers to interracial adoption. The issue arose because the number of black children looking for adoptive parents far outnumbered the number of available black families. The National Association of Black Social Workers termed interracial adoption "cultural genocide" and backed the efforts of a number of states to establish preferences for same-race adoptions, with the result that large numbers of black children languished in foster care.

The institute's main case in the area was on behalf of Scott and Lou Ann Mullen, who tried to adopt two young black children, Matthew and Joseph. Scott was white and Lou Ann was American Indian, and they were raising a multiracial family. As foster parents, the Mullens had taken Matthew, who was born to a mother infected with syphilis and addicted to crack cocaine, into their home when he was four days old. They nursed him to health and, when he turned two, tried to adopt him and his older brother. Instead, the Texas Department of Protective and Regulatory Services removed Matthew from their home because of race and placed both boys in a black adoptive home, where the placement failed. The boys were then placed in an orphanage.

The lawsuit attracted national coverage and support across ideological lines. The Institute for Justice teamed with Harvard law professors Laurence Tribe, Randall Kennedy, and Elizabeth Bartholet to challenge the state's discriminatory practices. The state responded by passing a law making it a crime for social workers to discriminate in adoption placements. (Bolick calls it the "send a social worker to jail" law.) Soon thereafter, federal legislation sponsored by Senator Howard Metzenbaum (D–OH) was enacted, banning discrimination in adoption placements.

In 1998, Bolick authored *The Affirmative Action Fraud: How to Restore the American Civil Rights Vision*,[2] which argues that racial preferences create a harmful cosmetic illusion of racial progress that obscures serious problems—particularly a growing racial academic gap—that remain unaddressed. With the emergence of other conservative groups devoted to fighting racial preferences, the Institute for Justice has turned its focus exclusively to empowerment issues.

THE CENTER FOR LEGAL AND JUDICIAL STUDIES

Since its founding more than 30 years ago, The Heritage Foundation has worked to bring like-minded conservatives and market-based thinkers together to promote a shared mission and mutual goals. Since 1977, for example, Heritage has hosted an annual Resource Bank conference to help build a coalition devoted to free-market principles. Resource Bank meetings bring together important policy activists who can help implement those principles. The bank now includes about 450 individuals from 232 organizations (including 96 CEOs) from 25 countries.

The work of the Center for Legal and Judicial Studies, begun by Heritage in 2000, is a natural outgrowth of Heritage's coalition-building activities. Chaired by former Attorney General Edwin Meese III, the center sponsors meetings attended by the CEOs of the nation's leading freedom-based public interest legal organizations. At these meetings, groups share information on legal developments, discuss responses to common problems, and exchange ideas on management issues. The meetings also facilitate increased cooperation on issues of mutual interest, including the filing of *amicus curiae* (friend of the court) briefs in key cases.

With help from Heritage's Director of Coalition Relations and events like the Resource Bank, the Center for Legal and Judicial Studies also helps to promote cooperation between the freedom-based public interest legal groups and state policy groups and other public policy think tanks. The effort to promote and defend school choice programs is a good example of this collaborative effort. Public policy groups have produced valuable research on the benefits of school choice and information on implementation of the programs that is relevant in some litigation. Public interest legal groups have provided legal advice on the best ways to structure school choice programs to withstand a legal challenge and also have defended them in litigation that has reached the Supreme Court.

To promote additional cooperation among freedom-based public interest law organizations and other policy groups, the center, directed by Todd Gaziano, also hosts a monthly meeting for Washington, D.C.-based legal groups and other area organizations with a legal component. The meetings include a discussion of current legal and public policy developments and occasionally include participation by government officials.

The Center for Legal and Judicial Studies also has a Supreme Court advocacy program that includes Supreme Court e-mail alerts, *amicus curiae* brief conferences, and mock oral argument sessions. Because of its proximity to the Supreme Court building, the center can collect every opinion and order as soon as it is released. Within an hour, the center sends an e-mail alert to public interest leaders summarizing the Court's action. This provides subscribers with accurate and timely information, helping them to respond with press releases and commentary that help news organizations make better sense of the legal meaning and impact of the Court's decisions.

At the request of an attorney or freedom-based public interest organization, the center periodically hosts *amicus curiae* conferences and special issue conferences, in person and over the Internet. The meetings help the lead counsel in important cases to develop ideas for *amicus* briefs. They also allow the counsel to communicate the need for such briefs to interested organizations. If the Supreme Court of the United States agrees to hear a case of national importance, the center will volunteer to organize a mock session of Supreme Court oral arguments ("moot court") to help the public interest advocate prepare for his appearance before the high court. Such realistic moot courts with leading Supreme Court lawyers help the oral advocates sharpen their argument. The center's guest oral advocates have won a number of difficult cases by 5 to 4 decisions, reinforcing the opinion of many that the rigorous moot courts made a difference.

In addition to working directly with public interest legal groups, scholars at the Center for Legal and Judicial Studies provide intellectual support for freedom-based legal reform and fidelity to constitutional government. The center and its individual scholars—such as senior legal research fellow Paul Rosenzweig—publish papers, law review and magazine articles, and op-ed newspaper essays. The scholars also testify before Congress and similar bodies, and appear in television and radio broadcasts to promote the rule of law and our constitutional system.

Priority issues include federalism, separation of powers, the proper role of the judiciary, equality under law, religious liberty, civil justice reform, crime control and public safety, and guaranteed liberties. Through such efforts, the center seeks to educate citizens and policymakers on the history, true meaning, and continuing importance of our Constitution and legal traditions. This work, in turn, reinforces the litigation in the *true* public interest undertaken by the freedom-based public interest law movement.

Todd Gaziano

Southeastern Legal Foundation

Southeastern Legal Foundation, founded in 1976, is among the nation's first and oldest public interest law firms and policy centers. The foundation's purpose is to advance limited government and individual rights under the guidance and protection of the Constitution. In two primary areas of activity—government contracting programs and public university admissions—its commitment to equality without preference and prejudice is in plain view.

In 1992, the foundation argued successfully before the Supreme Court on behalf of the Associated General Contractors of Northeastern Florida, challenging an unconstitutional set-aside program for public contracting in the city of Jacksonville. The decision, the first high court opinion written by Justice Clarence Thomas, was a critical victory in ensuring that plaintiffs who want to challenge preferences based on race, ethnicity, and sex in government contracting programs have legal standing to do so.

In 1998, the foundation filed suit against the city of Atlanta, which had maintained a quota system for its contracts for a quarter-century. After bitter and much publicized controversy, the city dismantled its program and settled with the plaintiffs. The case received national attention because it brought to light the corruption involved in the implementation of these programs—specifically, how the programs encourage the start-up of "front companies" that pose as minority-owned businesses but really exist only to meet the quota required by the government.

In 1998, the foundation also challenged DeKalb County's system of limiting its student transfers based on race. On behalf of students who were not allowed to transfer to a school of choice because of their race, the foundation challenged the program, and the county agreed to settle the case and drop the program, moving to a race-neutral program designed to relieve overcrowding in the schools generally. In 1999, the foundation challenged a Nashville, Tennessee, magnet school program with a racial quota requirement of 30 percent minority students. The Nashville School District settled the case and adopted a race-neutral lottery system for entry.

In early 2002, Southeastern Legal Foundation represented a minority-owned firm that bid as a prime contractor on a construction project for the city of Charlotte, North Carolina. Even though the client would have been eligible to bid as a preferred subcontractor, when he bid as a prime contractor, he was required to give away a portion of his work to minority business enterprises listed by the city. When he was not able to find enough minority contractors to do the work, he lost the job. Because the law in this area was so clear, when the foundation filed a complaint the city settled the case, agreeing to drop the program and provide for race-neutral programs to help all small businesses get work with the city.

Mountain States Legal Foundation

One of the greatest contributions to ending racial quotas and preferences in government contracting came from what might have seemed an unlikely source. Mountain States Legal Foundation had been created in 1977 in response to the "Sagebrush Rebellion" in which Westerners objected to the restrictions placed on their ability to engage in economic and recreational activity on federal lands. Accordingly, the foundation focused on natural resources and environmental laws.

With the Supreme Court's approval of racial quotas and preferences in government contracting in *Fullilove v. Klutznick*, however, Congress was emboldened to expand, and state and local governments felt empowered to enact, race-based contracting programs—and organizations like Mountain States soon had a new call upon their services by non-minority contractors who were denied jobs because of their race.

The foundation concluded, after an initial, unsuccessful lawsuit initiated in 1987, that a challenge to the ability of states to award highway contracts on the basis of race might be more successful if it were directed not at the states' implementation of the federal program, but at the underlying federal program itself. This was easier said than done; most highway construction contracts are awarded by the states and not by the federal government.

In late 1989, however, Randy and Valery Pech of Colorado Springs, Colorado, approached the foundation. Mr. Pech's tiny company, Adarand Constructors, Inc., had bid to install the guardrail along five miles of federal highway in the San Juan

National Forest in Dolores and Montezuma counties in south-western Colorado. Although he had submitted the lowest bid and had an excellent reputation for doing high-quality work on a timely basis, his bid was rejected because the federal agency in charge of building highways on federal lands had awarded the prime contractor a $10,000 bidding bonus for awarding the guardrail subcontract to a minority-owned company.

In August 1990, the Mountain States Legal Foundation filed the lawsuit for Adarand Constructors, Inc., in federal district court and began a long and convoluted journey through the federal court system. Ultimately, Adarand would appear on three occasions before the U.S. Supreme Court.

By far the most significant of these visits occurred on January 17, 1995, when William Perry Pendley, the foundation's president and chief legal officer, argued for Adarand. Pendley did a superb job. On June 12, 1995, the Court issued its ruling in Adarand's favor, holding that there was no difference between what the Constitution demanded of state and local governments, as set forth in *Croson*, and what it required of the federal government. *Adarand* was sent back with instructions for the lower courts to conduct fact finding and to issue a new ruling consistent with the Supreme Court's ruling.

It is difficult to overstate the importance of the Supreme Court's 1995 *Adarand* ruling. *Time*, for example, declared: "[I]t was Rehnquist's court that ruled in [*Adarand*] in 1995 that preferential treatment based on race in government programs is almost always unconstitutional. This was a legal earthquake, throwing into doubt most of the government's affirmative action programs."[3]

On its return to Colorado federal courts, after lengthy discovery demanded by the Clinton administration, *Adarand* prevailed when the federal district court ruled in 1997 that the federal program failed "strict scrutiny" for lack of "narrow tailoring." In 1999, the

Tenth Circuit held that the *Adarand* case was moot in a ruling that was reversed by a *per curiam* decision of the Supreme Court in January 2000.

In September 2002, the Tenth Circuit then reversed the district court's opinion on the merits, upholding the constitutionality of the federal highway construction program. The Supreme Court granted Adarand's petition for review in March 2001, but, in response to dubious arguments made by the Bush administration that the federal program had been changed to such a degree that Adarand was no longer injured, then dismissed Adarand's petition as having been granted "improvidently." The decision was a clear setback for opponents of racial preferences and quotas.

In January 1992, a little more than a year after filing the Adarand lawsuit, the Mountain States Legal Foundation filed a lawsuit on behalf of a small family-owned company, Concrete Works of Colorado, and its owner and operator, Marc Lenart, challenging a race-based contracting program used by the city and county of Denver since 1983. Like *Adarand*, the company's case had a tortuous trip through the federal courts, and, also like *Adarand*, it prevailed when a Colorado federal district court declared Denver's program unconstitutional.

When Denver appealed, however, the Tenth Circuit used its ruling in *Adarand*, which the Supreme Court, at the behest of the Bush administration, had left standing, to reverse the district court's ruling in the Concrete Works of Colorado case. In November 2003, the Supreme Court, over a strong dissent by Justice Antonin Scalia in which Chief Justice William Rehnquist concurred, declined to hear the case.

Meanwhile, the foundation became involved in another racial issue—the demand by Clinton administration lawyers under the leadership of Bill Lann Lee that Western rural counties racially gerrymander their commissioner districts to guarantee election of minority candidates. (Many Western states require election of commissioners at large from residential districts.) Using Section 2 of the Voting Rights Act, the Department of Justice demanded that Blaine County, Montana, gerrymander its districts to ensure election of an American Indian commissioner despite the absence of evidence that anyone had ever been prevented from registering, voting, or running for office in Blaine County on the basis of race. Clinton administration lawyers prepared a similar case against Alamosa County, Colorado, demanding racial gerrymandering for local Hispanics, a lawsuit that the Bush administration then filed it its earliest days. Mountain States Legal Foundation won in *United States v. Alamosa County, Colorado*, and *United States v. Blaine County, Montana* is en route to the Supreme Court.

Washington Legal Foundation

The Washington Legal Foundation, based in the District of Columbia, played a leading role in the *Podberesky* case, described below, and has filed *amicus* briefs in 20 or 30 important civil rights cases over the years, including key briefs in two other cases also discussed below.

Podberesky v. Kirwan. The Washington Legal Foundation first got involved in race-based scholarship issues in 1990–91, filing a series of complaints with the Department of Education regarding schools that offered race-exclusive scholarships. The foundation's efforts in this area brought it to the attention of Daniel Podberesky, then a freshman at the University of Maryland-College Park, who had been denied a Banneker Scholarship because it was open only to blacks. While Podberesky is Hispanic, he asked only that he be considered for a scholarship without regard to race. Podberesky filed suit against the university, alleging violations of Title VI and the Equal Protection Clause, and, after an adverse trial court ruling, the foundation took over the case and won before the Fourth Circuit.

The combination of *Podberesky* and *Hopwood v. Texas* (a Center for Individual Rights case, discussed above) pretty much ended efforts by the education establishment to justify racial preferences as necessary to overcome past discrimination. If Maryland and the University of Texas, two schools with strict segregationist pasts, could not win on those grounds, it was clear that no one else could. Thereafter, schools were forced to rely solely on diversity rationales.

Shaw v. Reno. The Voting Rights Act Amendments of 1982 eliminated "discriminatory intent" as a necessary element in establishing a violation of Section 2 of the Voting Rights Act. As a result, the civil rights establishment began to press its view that failure to maximize the number of majority-minority voting districts within a state violated the Voting Rights Act because such a failure could be said to have a "discriminatory result" for racial minority groups. During the first Bush administration, the Justice Department's Civil Rights Division adopted that view and succeeded in pressuring several Southern states into adopting redistricting plans that maximized majority-minority voting districts.

A number of North Carolina citizens challenged such a plan as a violation of the Equal Protection Clause (as well as the Fifteenth Amendment). The Washington Legal Foundation became involved in the case after a three-judge district court panel rejected the challenge. The plaintiffs were white citizens who complained that, by creating a district with the express purpose of ensuring the election of a black candidate, state officials denied them (as white voters) equal voting rights. The foundation was concerned that if the case was focused on discrimination against white voters, the Supreme Court might not be willing to overturn the redistricting plan. It therefore filed a brief that focused instead on the right of all citizens to live in a society in which the government does not segregate voters on the basis of race.

In June 1993, the Supreme Court issued a 5 to 4 decision in *Shaw v. Reno* that largely mirrored the approach taken in the foundation's brief (which was joined by the Equal Opportunity Foundation, the Center for Equal Opportunity's predecessor). Indeed, the central focus of Justice Sandra Day O'Connor's decision was *Wright v. Rockefeller*, particularly Justice William O. Douglas's dissenting opinion in that case; the foundation brief focused heavily on *Wright*, while the case was not cited in any other brief filed in *Shaw*.

The Washington Legal Foundation also participated in several of the Supreme Court cases that were follow-ups to *Shaw*, and it is fair to say that it played a large role in shaping the Supreme Court's jurisprudence in the area.

Alexander v. Sandoval. Title VI of the Civil Rights Act of 1964 prohibits a recipient of federal funding from discriminating on the basis of race, color, or national origin. In *Guardians Association v. Civil Service Commission of New York*, the Supreme Court held that a Title VI claim requires proof of discriminatory intent. But some years before *Guardians* was decided, federal agencies (at the insistence of the Justice Department) had issued regulations stating that recipients of federal funds are also prohibited from engaging in conduct that has a discriminatory "effect" on the basis of race, color, or national origin. *Guardians* includes language that can be used either to support or to challenge the validity of the disparate effect regulations.

Although that issue has never been addressed directly by the Supreme Court, the federal appeals courts responded to *Guardians* by unanimously finding that the Title VI regulations were valid and prohibited both intentional discrimination and conduct having a disparate impact on protected groups. Washington Legal Foundation attorneys wrote several articles in the 1980s and 1990s attacking the validity of the disparate impact regulations, but they made no headway in the federal appeals courts.

For many years, the Title VI regulations had a devastating impact in several areas. The regulations gave rise to the so-called environmental justice movement, for example, under which plaintiffs can fight economic development on the ground that the projects will have an adverse environmental impact on the community and that the community has a larger percentage of some racial minority group than some other community not facing a similar impact. Moreover, fear of disparate impact litigation invariably leads government officials to adopt racial quotas (whether in hiring, school admissions, or government contracts) as a means of heading off such litigation. Use of testing in school admissions became extremely problematic because some racial groups often perform better on such tests than do other racial groups.

In 2000, the Supreme Court granted review in *Alexander v. Sandoval*, in which the Eleventh Circuit had held that Alabama's policy of giving driver license tests only in English violated the Title VI regulations because the policy had a disparate impact on the basis of national origin. The foundation's brief on the merits (and another brief filed by the Pacific Legal Foundation and the Center for Equal Opportunity) argued strongly that the disparate impact regulations were invalid because they went beyond Title VI's authority.

The Supreme Court ultimately overturned the Eleventh Circuit's decision. Not surprisingly, the Court did not directly address the validity of the regulations. Nonetheless, Justice Scalia's majority opinion contains broad language suggesting that the regulations are inconsistent with Title VI itself and, therefore, that there is doubt about the regulations' validity. That decision will permit litigants to revisit the issue of the regulations' validity in the lower courts. A major reason that the Court was unwilling to discern a congressional intent to create a private right of action was that the regulations are so at odds with the provisions of Title VI—a disparity that the Washington Legal Foundation and the other groups focused on throughout their briefs.

Individual Rights Foundation

The Individual Rights Foundation is the legal arm of the Los Angeles-based Center for the Study of Popular Culture. Its general counsel, Manny Klausner, has been engaged in complex and significant constitutional, election law, and business litigation matters for four decades.

In 1996, Klausner participated in the campaign to pass the California Civil Rights Initiative (Proposition 209). He assisted in drafting Proposition 209 and served as vice chairman, with Ward Connerly as chairman, of the "Yes-on-209" campaign. Klausner and Patrick Manshardt, a lawyer with the foundation until 2003, served as public spokesmen for the initiative. Klausner also represented the proponents of Proposition 209 in the district court and the Ninth Circuit in *Coalition for Economic Equity v. Wilson*, the case discussed above which upheld the constitutionality of Proposition 209.

The Individual Rights Foundation has been involved in many cases challenging governmental racial preferences and other governmental abuses. In *Tipton-Whittingham v. Los Angeles*, the ACLU and the NAACP Legal Defense Fund, led by Bill Lann Lee—who went on to head the Justice Department's Civil Rights Division under President Bill Clinton—tried to do an end run around Proposition 209 by attempting to obtain the signature of a magistrate judge to a consent decree that would have saddled the Los Angeles Police Department with race- and gender-based preferences for the next 18 years.

Lee and his colleagues never informed Judge William Keller, the district court judge to whom the case was assigned, that they would be referring the case to a magistrate judge for her signature on the consent decree on the day of Proposition 209's passage. Their hope was that the magistrate judge would sign the consent decree before Proposition 209 became law so that the preferences in the consent decree would have come within Proposition 209's express exception for consent decrees that pre-existed its passage.

The week before Proposition 209 was passed, however, Manshardt co-wrote an op-ed essay in the *Los Angeles Times* that blew the whistle on Lee's (and the city's) attempted end run. When Judge Keller read it, he pulled the case from the magistrate judge. Shortly thereafter, Klausner and Manshardt were permitted to intervene in the case on behalf of a white police lieutenant, Richard Dyer. The

ACLU eventually dropped its request for a consent decree after the organization recognized that Keller wouldn't sign it.

In early 1997, the Individual Rights Foundation lawyers then represented Lieutenant Dyer in his own action against the city of Los Angeles for race discrimination regarding Dyer's efforts to obtain a watch commander position with the police department's Air Support Division. The case went to trial, and Judge Keller found that the city had conducted a sham job selection process: It had already decided to hire a less-qualified black supervisor before the process had even taken place; otherwise, a white candidate— although not Dyer—would have been selected for the position. Because Dyer had in fact been unlawfully discriminated against because of his race, Keller awarded him $20,000 for emotional distress plus his attorneys' fees.

Shortly after Judge Keller's award to Dyer, police management began a campaign of retaliation. Dyer applied a few more times for the position at the Air Support Division, and each time lesser-qualified candidates were hired. Finally, in December 2000, the foundation's lawyers again filed suit on behalf of Dyer against the city, this time for the police department's retaliation. The city eventually settled Dyer's lawsuit. He is currently the watch commander at the Air Support Division and received his helicopter pilot's wings in November 2003.

In September 2000, the foundation turned its sights on race-based preferences in the Los Angeles Fire Department, representing David Alexander, a paramedic who was denied a job as a firefighter because of a 1974 consent decree's "residency requirement," which required all applicants to the fire department to be residents of the city of Los Angeles from the time of their application throughout probation. The residency requirement's purpose was specifically to limit the number of whites in the applicant pool. In July 2001, the city settled Alexander's case and hired him as a firefighter with the department.

Two new white firefighters, Richard Hurst and Shawn Phillips, picked up Alexander's mantle and continued the challenge to the 1974 consent decree, which also included de facto quotas. In April 2002, when they realized that a ruling on the foundation's challenge could not be blocked, the United States and the city agreed to end the 28-year-old consent decree. In April 2003, the Individual Rights Foundation, with Alexander and another white firefighter applicant, Robert Smollen, successfully challenged the city of Los Angeles' affirmative action program, which was declared unconstitutional by Los Angeles Superior Court Judge Helen Bendix.

Center for Equal Opportunity

The Center for Equal Opportunity, headed by Linda Chavez, is not, strictly speaking, a public interest *litigation* organization, but it has played such an important role in fighting racial and ethnic preferences since its inception in 1995 that its activities should be discussed here.

Along with the Sacramento-based American Civil Rights Institute, which has pushed for ballot initiatives all over the country to end the use of racial and ethnic preferences and classifications by government, CEO has challenged the racially exclusive programs at approximately 100 universities. In these challenges, it has demanded that the programs be opened up to all students regardless of skin color or ethnicity—or else it will file a complaint with the U.S. Department of Education's Office for Civil Rights. The overwhelming majority of schools to which CEO has written (e.g., Princeton, the University of Delaware, University of Virginia, Iowa State, and the University of Texas) have responded favorably.

Prior to this project, CEO challenged racially exclusive scholarships at schools in the U.S. Court of Appeals for the Fourth Circuit, which had particularly favorable case law in light of the *Podberesky* decision (discussed above), with favorable results there as well. North Carolina passed legislation; Virginia and South Carolina changed scholarships administratively. In a related initiative, the University of Maryland ended a women-only scholarship program after CEO challenged it.

The Center for Equal Opportunity has also filed several complaints with the Office for Civil Rights about the use of racial and ethnic preferences in admissions. The first was filed against Rice University; CEO shared this complaint with the University of Texas and Texas A&M, since they had also been declaring a desire to return to using preferences. CEO also filed a complaint against Texas Tech when it, too, announced a decision to revert to preferences. Most recently, in late 2003, CEO filed complaints with the Education Department against a medical school (the University of Maryland); a pair of law schools (at the University of Virginia and at William & Mary); and a statewide undergraduate system of campuses (the University of North Carolina system). These complaints were based on earlier CEO studies that documented strong evidence of severe racial and ethnic admission preferences at the schools.

CEO recently concluded that simply requiring universities to reveal the extent to which they use preferences is a good way to discourage and limit such discrimination. Accordingly, it has drafted model state legislation for the American Legislative Exchange Council (ALEC), an influential national group of conservative state legislators, and freedom-of-information requests for the National Association of Scholars that would require schools to reveal whether and how race is weighed in admissions. In late 2003, CEO met with relevant U.S. Senate committee staff to discuss similar legislation by Congress. Earlier, it drafted model legislation for ALEC that cloned Proposition 209; ALEC is still using this model bill. CEO also helped particular legislators draft bills that would ban preferences in Virginia and New Hampshire.

In the recent University of Michigan affirmative action cases, CEO lobbied hard to get the Bush administration to file a brief opposing preferences, with some success. The CEO's *amicus* briefs in the Michigan cases focused specifically on why diversity is not a compelling governmental interest and highlighted the many CEO state-by-state studies that documented the use of racial preferences. CEO's California studies preceded and provided support for Proposition 209; its Washington study preceded and provided support for a similar, and likewise successful, initiative there.

At the K–12 level, the Center for Equal Opportunity contacted dozens of school districts in Florida that were using different I.Q. test cutoffs for gifted and talented programs, depending on race; as a result, first the districts and then the state itself agreed to end the practice. It sent letters to all federal trial judges with pending desegregation orders (several hundred), urging them to dismiss racial-balancing requirements if *de jure* segregation had been eliminated; many judges responded favorably to this request.

CEO has worked to challenge preferences in areas outside of the educational arena as well. The Federalist Society's civil rights practice group, chaired by CEO's general counsel Roger Clegg, has prepared an index of all state racial classifications—particularly contracting preferences—that will be posted on its Web site. This project grew out of the "All Deliberate Speed" project letters from Linda Chavez, Clint Bolick, Ward Connerly, and Ed Meese to state attorneys general regarding state racial and ethnic classifications, as well as CEO's follow-up visits to various states to speak about this issue to local Federalist Society chapters. CEO has already added a section to its Web site to facilitate legal challenges to contracting preferences by private parties. The Web site provides similar resources for those who wish to challenge stale desegregation decrees and disparate impact rules and regulations.

The Center for Equal Opportunity monitors federal legislation that contains racial classifications and meets with congressional staff, urges administration opposition, and helps to organize outside opponents. The group has challenged the use of racial and ethnic preferences by a wide range of employers, including Fortune Brands, American University, Lawrence Livermore Laboratories,

Virginia Tech, and the Kentucky State Board of Education. It has also been in constant contact with the different parts of the federal government that deal with employment matters involving racial and ethnic preferences.

CEO, for instance, has met with top officials at the Labor Department and drafted proposed changes in its regulations under Executive Order 11,246 that encourage private contractors to use such preferences. Finally, CEO coordinated a systematic letter-writing campaign to state legislators and other critical players in the redistricting process after the 2000 Census, pointing out the legal infirmities with racial gerrymandering and including a formal CEO-commissioned legal analysis on the subject.

Other Organizations

Other litigating organizations in the freedom-based public interest legal movement have made critical contributions to the struggle against preferences based on race, ethnicity, and sex. The Atlantic Legal Foundation, for example, recently succeeded in forcing New Jersey to abandon its use of public contracting preferences in *GEOD Corporation v. New Jersey*. Because of New Jersey's "affirmative action" programs, a substantial percentage of its construction contracts had been awarded to minority-owned firms. The foundation's client, in many cases, was not even permitted to bid. Its specialized work had been "carved out" by prime contractors for minority firms, enabling the prime contractor to satisfy the obligation to utilize minority subcontractors.

New Jersey's disparity study was based on 15-year-old census data, which the foundation argued were too old to be a proper basis for a lawful affirmative action program. It also maintained that census data are inherently inadequate because they do not provide information about the ability or willingness of minority and women-owned firms to perform state construction contracts (criteria which the Supreme Court deemed essential in *City of Richmond v. J.A. Croson Co.*).

The state indicated a willingness to settle the litigation, and in July 2003, Judge Stanley Chesler of the U.S. District Court for New Jersey signed a consent degree in which the state signed a permanent injunction against enforcement of those provisions of the state's Set-Aside Act that allow the state to set aside contracts for or establish contract goals for minority-owned or women-owned business enterprises. To achieve disadvantaged-business enterprise goals on federally funded projects, New Jersey must use race-neutral means to the maximum extent possible. Finally, the state's submissions to the U.S. Department of Transportation must be vetted by GEOD and the Atlantic Legal Foundation before submission. After the consent decree was entered, New Jersey's attorney general conceded that "this set-aside program could not survive constitutional scrutiny."[4] The foundation and its client had every reason to celebrate their total victory.

As a follow-up to *GEOD v. New Jersey*, the Atlantic Legal Foundation is preparing to bring a lawsuit against New Jersey Transit, a public corporation that owns and operates commuter rail lines and consumer bus lines. The corporation's own disparity study shows that firms owned by one presumptively "disadvantaged" group—Asian–Americans—are "overutilized" while firms owned by another "disadvantaged" group—women—are "underutilized" by such a small degree as to be statistically insignificant. The foundation intends to straighten out New Jersey Transit's "affirmative action" practices, pointing out, among other things, that federal guidelines require race-neutral means to the greatest extent possible to produce participation by disadvantaged business enterprises.

Demonstrating the importance of perseverance, Atlantic Legal Foundation worked for a decade to invalidate New York City's racial quotas program in the awarding of city contracts. It launched a multi-pronged attack in New York state and federal courts in *North Shore Concrete v. City of New York*, *Halmar Cor-*

poration v. City of New York, and *Seabury Construction Corp. v. City of New York*. Each case was based on a different legal theory, challenging the city's program as violating (1) the federal Constitution's Equal Protection Clause; (2) the state constitution's equal protection clause; and (3) the state's requirement that municipal contracts be awarded to the lowest qualified bidder. The campaign ended with the city's agreement to suspend the program, allow it to lapse, and pay substantial legal fees and costs.

Non-litigating organizations have likewise played an important role. Publications of the National Legal Center for the Public Interest and debates sponsored by the Federalist Society have focused on the use of classifications and preferences based on race, ethnicity, and sex. The Heritage Foundation, the Cato Institute, the Manhattan Institute, Project 21, and the Center for New Black Leadership each have made important contributions as well.

Conclusion

The freedom-based public interest law movement's contributions to the struggle against preferences and discrimination based on race, ethnicity, and sex have been enormous. This is an area with lasting consequences for all Americans. But it is also one in which, for a variety of reasons, the political, economic, and legal marketplaces have failed to protect Americans' interests.

Fortunately, the organizations discussed in this chapter have filled this gap. As a result, the development of the case law in this area—while admittedly not perfect and still evolving—protects the rights of millions more Americans.

---

[1] New Brunswick, N.J.: Transaction Publishers.

[2] Oakland, Cal.: Institute for Contemporary Studies.

[3] "How Rehnquist Changed America," *Time*, June 30, 2003.

[4] Kathy Barrett, "State Has to Drop Set-Aside Program," *Newark Star-Ledger*, July 12, 2003.

CHAPTER 7

Freedom of Speech for All

Thor L. Halvorssen

The majority of free speech cases litigated from the 1920s through the Vietnam War at the Supreme Court level involved the rights of radical dissidents: U.S. Communist Party members, anti-war protesters, members of the labor movement, journalists, and white supremacists.[1] The American Civil Liberties Union was the most powerful actor in these free speech struggles, and its work ensured that First Amendment protections expanded rapidly throughout the 20th century.

The past 30 years, however, have seen a dramatic political shift in the nature of First Amendment cases. While early First Amendment cases involved securing the free speech rights of radicals, much recent litigation has been brought by new constituencies.

Since the 1970s, courts have heard cases in which the plaintiffs include members of mainstream groups and political parties as well as people of faith, pro-life activists, and conservative advocates. In many of these instances, litigants have tried to enlarge the scope of freedom. In others, they have fought against official attempts to censor unpopular or "ideologically incorrect" ideas.

The architects of many landmark cases have come from the freedom-based public interest law movement.

The mid-1970s saw the emergence of a number of groups that organized themselves tactically in much the same way as the ACLU, but that espoused conservative and libertarian ideals. On matters of free speech, these new organizations sought both to add conservative and classical liberal voices to cases where there could be cooperation across the political spectrum and to oppose the ACLU and other public interest legal groups such as the National Organization for Women and the Mexican American Legal Defense and Educational Fund where these groups had abandoned or even opposed freedom of speech in the name of advancing civil rights.

One may see the centrality of the ACLU's role and its influence in shaping the freedom-based legal movement when one considers the fact that two of the movement's important groups—the American Civil Rights Union and American Center for Law and Justice—were created precisely to counterbalance it.

Over the past three decades, organizations spawned by the freedom-based public interest law movement have played significant roles in protecting the freedom of speech of all Americans. Some of these groups, such as the Atlantic Legal Foundation and Mountain States Legal Foundation, initially organized themselves geographically; others, such as the Becket Fund for Religious Liberty and Americans United for Life, oriented themselves around specific political issues.

Most cases in the movement's efforts to protect freedom of speech have occurred in the arena of education. At the primary and secondary school level, organizations have done much to expand religious students' free speech rights. At the college level, the movement has made successful but intermittent efforts to prevent universities from persecuting and prosecuting students and faculty who do not conform to left-wing authoritarianism in the form of ideological correctness.

When colleges and universities began to introduce speech codes at campuses across the country—with disastrous consequences for an educational environment that depends on the free flow of ideas—the movement's attorneys successfully challenged and eliminated a small number of these codes. Hundreds remain intact, but the past three years have seen renewed interest in the movement's pro-freedom efforts as universities increasingly have used these codes to violate students' and faculty members' First Amendment rights.

In the arena of political protest, the movement has made contributions in important cases involving the freedom of speech rights of both pro-life protesters and political extremists. Movement attorneys have litigated against compelled speech: The First Amendment protects the individual's right to speak his own mind but also protects the individual from being forced to express opinions, ideas, or ideological viewpoints that he does not believe or wish to uphold.

In school voucher cases, movement attorneys have defended freedom of association and freedom of speech in upholding parents' rights to choose a religious school when they consider it best for their children's educational needs. The movement has produced a string of victories for voluntary association, an essential aspect of freedom of expression, in virtually every arena of American life, from primary school and universities to civic organizations and clubs such as the Boy Scouts. In matters of electoral politics, the movement is engaged now and for the foreseeable future in challenging the indefensible restrictions on freedom of speech masked as "campaign finance reform."

It is not possible in this short essay to catalogue and credit the extraordinary work of the approximately three dozen litigating organizations that comprise the freedom-based public interest law movement. By litigating; funding and coordinating private-sector litigators; writing friend of the court briefs; educating law student interns; and contributing to the public agenda through debates, conferences, and effective media impact, these groups have achieved immeasurable results in American public law and public policy.

This chapter will therefore highlight major free speech victories at the Supreme Court level and note a number of cases at the circuit, district, and even state levels that are considered to be turning points in the recent history of freedom of speech.

Voluntary Associations

The separation of church and state is a principle enshrined in America's founding documents. For decades, school officials used this justification to deny religious students, primarily Christians, equal treatment. While all manner of student clubs—from environmental clubs to gay-straight alliances—could use public school facilities for their after-school meetings, schools routinely denied that right to religious groups on the grounds that granting it would constitute state sponsorship of religion.

Critics, however, noted that free speech is meaningless when students are denied the right to organize around shared beliefs. Voluntary association, although not specifically mentioned in the First Amendment, is a right implied by the right to "peaceably assemble."

In 1990, the Supreme Court ruled that voluntarily organized religious activities by children at an Omaha, Nebraska, public high school constituted private speech and, as such, were not forbidden by the Establishment Clause of the First Amendment. The case, *Board of Education v. Mergens*, was a significant victory because it solidified a concept more than ten years in the making.

The case began in 1985 when a student, Bridget Mergens, was denied use of the Westside High School facilities for an extracurricular student Bible study group. Jay Sekulow, who subsequently became chief counsel of the American Center for Law and Justice, served as lead counsel in the Supreme Court and presented the oral argument that all students, including religious students, enjoy the constitutional guarantee of free speech. The Court agreed.

The ruling in this case established the constitutionality of the 1984 Equal Access Act, which granted both non-religious and religious student groups the right to use school facilities after hours. The 1984 act was itself inspired by the Supreme Court's 1981 ruling in *Widmar v. Vincent*, in which an 8 to 1 majority held that if the University of Missouri was willing to permit secular student organizations to meet on campus, it must also allow Cornerstone, an organization of evangelical Christian students, the right to meet for worship and religious study.

The *Widmar* case was the basis of the *Mergens* decision. The movement made its presence felt in *Widmar* through an exceptionally important *amicus* brief contributed by the Center for Law and Religious Freedom of the Christian Legal Society.

Mergens was a key predecessor to one of the biggest triumphs for the American Center for Law and Justice. In 1993, the Court further expanded free speech protection to religious organizations in *Lamb's Chapel v. Center Moriches Union Free School District*. The case arose when Lamb's Chapel, a religious group seeking to screen a film featuring James Dobson of Focus on the Family, was denied access to the facilities of a New York public high school.

The American Center for Law and Justice argued that the Free Speech Clause of the First Amendment should trump the school district's erroneous claim that allowing Lamb's Chapel to use its facilities would have violated the Establishment Clause ban on government sponsorship of religion. The unanimous Supreme Court decision stated: "It discriminates on the basis of viewpoint to permit school property to be used for the presentation of all views about family issues and child-rearing except those dealing with the subject matter from a religious standpoint."

In 1997, the Good News Club, an evangelical Christian organization, sued in New York when it was denied the right to use the facilities of a public elementary school. *Good News Club v. Milford Central School* was litigated by the Virginia-based Rutherford Institute. In 2001, the Supreme Court definitively decided the matter of equal access when, writing for the majority, Justice Clarence Thomas explained that, even at the elementary school level, people of faith must be treated equally: "We find it quite clear that Milford engaged in viewpoint discrimination when it excluded the club from the after-school forum."

From *Widmar* to *Good News*, the movement had established the concept that, at every educational level, religious individuals and organizations cannot be denied their free speech and association rights. The movement's novel approach in these religious liberty cases was to argue that the issue of free speech should take precedence over mistaken concerns under the First Amendment's Establishment Clause.

In reaffirming viewpoint neutrality as a core tenet governing the use of public facilities, these Supreme Court decisions have altered the framework of American liberty. They are triumphs for everyone, not just for people of faith, as was seen when a public school in Alexandria, Louisiana, attempted to prevent an eleventh-grader from starting an after-school ACLU student club because the school principal believed that such a club would be divisive. Using these precedent-setting Supreme Court decisions, the student and his attorneys argued for his constitutional right to start the club.

What makes the American experiment such a wondrous phenomenon is the concept of equal justice under law. No citizen should enjoy fewer rights than any other.

Eliminating Viewpoint Discrimination

The freedom-based public interest law movement has also brought about extraordinary gains in preventing viewpoint discrimination against college student groups. In 1991, Ron Rosenberger, a student at the University of Virginia, sought funding from student government for a publication called *Wide Awake*. The student magazine was denied the requested $5,862 allocation because of its evangelical Christian viewpoint.

Rosenberger was told that the university, a state institution, could not fund "religious activity," even though the university was distributing funds to Muslim, Buddhist, Shinto, and Jewish student clubs. When the inconsistency was pointed out, the university explained that these religious groups were actually "cultural" organizations. Rosenberger then sued it for violating his First Amendment rights.

The case of *Rosenberger v. Rector* eventually made its way to the Supreme Court in 1995, where Michael W. McConnell and Michael P. McDonald of the Washington-based Center for Individual Rights argued for the plaintiff. Groups that filed *amicus curiae* briefs supporting Rosenberger's position included the American Center for Law and Justice, the Christian Legal Society, and the Intercollegiate Studies Institute, a conservative educational group that mentors alternative student journalists. On the other side, the ACLU wrote a brief arguing against the funding of religion on campus.

The Court ruled that not funding *Wide Awake* would constitute unconstitutional "viewpoint discrimination." The Court said, "Vital First Amendment speech principles are at stake here. The first danger to liberty lies in granting the state the power to examine publications to determine whether or not they are based on some ultimate idea and if so for the state to classify them."

"The viewpoint discrimination inherent in the university's regulation required public officials to scan and interpret student publications to discern their underlying philosophic assumptions respecting religious theory and belief," wrote Justice Anthony Kennedy. "That course of action was a denial of the right of free speech and would risk fostering a pervasive bias or hostility to religion, which could undermine the very neutrality the Establishment Clause requires. There is no Establishment Clause violation in the university's honoring its duties under the Free Speech Clause."

This decision meant that universities could no longer deny funds to students simply because they held religious or controversial points of view. One immediate result of the *Rosenberger* victory was felt within hours of the decision on the campus of the University of North Carolina-Chapel Hill. The student editor of the university's conservative newspaper received an unsolicited official communication from the chancellor informing him that, effective immediately, the conservative campus newspaper, long denied funding, was now eligible for funds.

Beyond the profound implications for freedom of speech on campus, the *Rosenberger* decision also paved the way for government-subsidized tuition vouchers for religious schools (*Zelman v. Simmons-Harris*, 2002), as discussed by Clint Bolick in Chapter 3.

THE CATO INSTITUTE'S CENTER FOR CONSTITUTIONAL STUDIES

The Cato Institute is a libertarian think tank that was founded in 1977 to broaden the national political debate. In 1989, Cato established its Center for Constitutional Studies under the direction of Roger Pilon to help revive and sustain the idea of limited constitutional government. The center's resident and adjunct scholars publish books, studies, articles, and op-ed newspaper essays. They lecture and debate, conduct conferences and policy and book forums, discuss legal issues of the day on TV and radio, and testify before Congress. In 1998, the center began filing *amicus curiae* briefs with the Supreme Court. In 2002, the center published its first annual *Cato Supreme Court Review*.

The climate of ideas from which the freedom-based public interest law movement emerged is often thought to have begun in 1944 with the publication of F. A.

Hayek's *The Road to Serfdom*. But the intellectual and political movement Hayek inspired has had two main strains: conservative, which traces its roots to Edmund Burke and the natural law tradition stretching back to antiquity, and libertarian, which traces its roots to John Locke and the natural rights tradition that grew from natural law and flourished during the Enlightenment.

Although conservatives and libertarians have much in common, differences have emerged over the role of the judiciary in our system of government. Both strains oppose the kind of judicial activism in which judges not only apply, but also make the law. Both believe that the Constitution limits the scope of governmental power, especially at the federal level, but they differ somewhat in their conceptions of the law to be applied.

Modern conservatives tend to read the Constitution as authorizing wider scope for majority rule than libertarians do. Thus, they often urge judicial deference to popular will, especially at the state level. Libertarians tend to read governmental power as more constrained, constitutionally—by the doctrine of enumerated powers at the federal level and by individual rights, both enumerated and unenumerated, in the case of both federal and state power. Thus, they urge judges to be "active" and to cite such sources to restrain governmental power.

This jurisprudential difference first emerged in the 1970s when conservatives began criticizing liberal judges for their expansive ideas about "rights." That set libertarians to the task of restoring the theory of rights that classical liberals had crafted, especially through the reason-based common law. Thus, in 1979, the Liberty Fund underwrote, through the Institute for Humane Studies, a seminal conference on the theory of rights, the proceedings of which appeared that year in the *Georgia Law Review*. A year later, the University of Chicago Press published Professor Bernard Siegan's magisterial *Economic Liberties and the Constitution*, which urged judges to be "active" in correcting the New Deal Supreme Court's reduction of economic liberties to a second-class status.

The debate between conservatives and libertarians continued at a 1984 Cato Institute conference in Washington on "Economic Liberties and the Judiciary." Then-Judge Antonin Scalia, reflecting the conservative view, recognized the importance of economic liberties but cautioned against judicial "activism" to secure such rights. The University of Chicago's Richard Epstein responded by calling on judges to enforce rights the Constitution was plainly written to protect, even if they had to repair to the theory and structure of the document to discover them.

The proceedings of the conference were published in the *Cato Journal* a year later and in a book by the George Mason University press two years after that, with a forward by Judge Alex Kozinski of the Ninth Circuit Court of Appeals. The conference led also to an American Bar Association bicentennial program on the subject in 1987 as well as a Federalist Society program that fall at the George Mason University Law School.

With the libertarian position on the role of the judiciary thus outlined, it remained for Cato to formally establish its Center for Constitutional Studies early in 1989. That year also saw the publication by Cato and the George Mason University Press of *The Rights Retained by the People*, an anthology on the history and meaning of the Ninth Amendment, edited by Boston University's Randy Barnett. From there it was a slow but steady effort to flesh out the Madisonian admonition that the judiciary should be "an impenetrable bulwark against every assumption of power in the Legislative or Executive."

That effort to articulate the Founders' vision of limited constitutional government, secured by an active but principled judiciary, involved two basic elements.

First, the doctrine of enumerated powers, which the Framers had meant to be the principal restraint on federal power, would need to be revived following its evisceration by the New Deal Court in 1937. That meant recasting federalism, which the Court under Chief Justice William Rehnquist had wanted to revive, not so much as dual sovereignty—and much less as "federal–state partnership," to say nothing of "states' rights"—but as delegated, enumerated, and thus limited powers, thereby capturing the Tenth Amendment's summation of the Constitution's theory of legitimacy. That effort culminated in 1994, six weeks before oral argument in *United States v. Lopez*, with the center's publication of a study by the University of Tennessee's Glenn Harlan Reynolds entitled *Kids, Guns, and the Commerce Clause: Is the Court Ready for Constitutional Government?*

Second, if both federal and state power were to be limited, the theory of rights that stands behind the Constitution would have to be articulated far better than the Court had managed to do over the years. On one hand, that theory was not an "open sesame," authorizing judges to discover whatever they wished. But on the other hand, neither were our rights limited to those enumerated in the document. The effort to articulate that theory has been an ongoing project of the center, taking many forms, but it reached fruition in 2003 with the Court's opinion in *Lawrence v. Texas*, which twice cited Cato's *amicus* brief. Speaking simply of liberty, the Court made it clear that the burden is on government to show why our liberty should be restricted. That presumption of liberty takes us to first principles. It is a mark of how the climate of ideas is changing.

Roger Pilon

Student Fees and Legal Equality

Student fees were first levied on some campuses more than a hundred years ago when universities across the country required students to pay a yearly fee to fund certain campus-wide activities. In the late 19th century, universities typically used these fees to pay for such things as diplomas, caps and gowns, and athletic equipment.

As campuses became political hotbeds in the 1960s and 1970s, many left-wing student leaders began using these funds to promote their political activities. Over the years, Ralph Nader's Public Interest Research Groups (PIRGs) collected millions of dollars from university student fees, using them to pursue a political agenda focused on consumer issues and the environment. Campus organizations increasingly used student fees to promote an ideologically liberal agenda that included abortion rights, gay and lesbian rights, and feminism.

Some students, believing it unfair that their fees were being used to promote viewpoints with which they disagreed, brought legal action. One of these cases made its way to the Supreme Court.

During the 1995–1996 academic year, a student at the Madison campus of the University of Wisconsin asked that he be allowed to opt out of paying a portion of his $331 student fee that funded the advocacy of student activist groups. Scott Southworth argued that it was unfair that he be forced to pay for the activities of groups whose viewpoints he abhorred, including the UW Greens, the International Socialist Organization, and the Campus Women's Center. Central to the First Amendment, he reasoned, is a right *not* to speak. When the University of Wisconsin refused to return his money, he sued.

The case received significant funding from the Alliance Defense Fund, an organization that has provided numerous grants in cases involving free speech rights. *Board of Regents v. Southworth*, argued at the Supreme Court in 1999 by Jordan Lorence, included *amicus* briefs from a number of movement organizations, such as the Atlantic Legal Foundation (which had previously litigated a crucial PIRG case in New York); the Pacific Legal Foundation; and the National Legal Foundation. Opposing *amicus* briefs were submitted by the ACLU, People for the American Way, and the National Education Association.

The Court agreed with Lorence that the fees involved Southworth's First Amendment rights and that he had a right not to fund groups he disagreed with if the university distributed such fees in a "viewpoint discriminatory" manner. Specifically, the "First Amendment permits a public university to charge its students an activity fee used to fund a program to facilitate extracurricular student speech *if the program is viewpoint neutral* [emphasis added]." Universities were now required, clearly and constitutionally, to use ironclad viewpoint neutrality when disbursing student fees. "When a university requires its students to pay fees to support the extracurricular speech of other students," Justice Kennedy wrote for the Court, "all in the interest of open discussion, it may not prefer some viewpoints to others."

The *Southworth* decision fit neatly with the *Rosenberger* decision and sent a clear message to universities: You may fund student groups, but you must do so in a fair and equitable manner. The effects of the *Southworth* decision are already manifest in the growth of a successful new cutting-edge environmental organization, Collegians for a Constructive Tomorrow (C-FACT), that counterbalances what it claims is the PIRGs' radical environmentalist agenda. C-FACT is seeking, with remarkable success, to obtain matching funds wherever the PIRGs receive student activity funding.

Whereas in *Southworth* the Supreme Court considered viewpoint-neutral disbursement of funds to be a good thing for university life, the Court had previously identified, in a fundamentally important case, a violation of the First Amendment through compelled speech. In 1990, the Supreme Court ruled unanimously in *Keller v. State Bar of California* that a bar association may not compel its members to pay a mandatory fee to support political or ideological activities that are not germane to practicing law or improving legal services. Twenty-one members of the California bar brought suit. Movement attorneys Anthony T. Caso, Ronald A. Zumbrun, and John H. Findley of the Pacific Legal Foundation represented the interests of the First Amendment in this case.

The foundation argued that the California bar's use of dues to lobby for gun control, a nuclear weapons freeze, and abortion rights was not germane to the purpose of regulating the legal profession or improving the quality of legal service and that it thus constituted compelled speech. Its case was supported by an *amicus* brief from the ACLU and established a nationwide procedure for attorneys to use in exercising their First Amendment rights. The case caused bar associations across the country to curtail their use of mandatory fees to fund political activism.

The Right to Be Politically Active

The constitutionally guaranteed right to engage in political activism and public protest has also been a movement priority. In 1994, attorneys from Liberty Counsel that were funded by the Alliance Defense Fund argued on behalf of the rights of pro-life activists protesting outside an abortion clinic. A bitterly divided Supreme Court ruled in *Madsen v. Women's Health Center, Inc.* that a Florida state court had not violated the First Amendment rights of a group of anti-abortion protesters when it created a "buffer zone" preventing them from approaching abortion clinics. Meanwhile, the Court struck down a 300-foot "no approach" zone and lifted restrictions on "images" (protest signs displaying pictures of aborted fetuses) that could be seen from inside the clinic. *Amicus* briefs were filed by Christian Legal Society, the American Center for Law and Justice, and the Rutherford Institute.

In *Schenck v. Pro-Choice Network of Western New York*, a 1997 American Center for Law and Justice case, the Supreme Court further clarified the First Amendment rights of abortion protesters by allowing a 15-foot "fixed buffer zone" but striking down a "floating buffer zone" that it deemed an unreasonable burden on free speech. In 2000, however, in *Hill v. Colorado*, the Court upheld a Colorado statute preventing any individual within 100 feet of an abortion facility's entrance from "knowingly approach[ing]" within eight feet of another person without that person's consent if the individual approached with the purpose of passing "a leaflet or handbill to, display a sign to, or engage in oral protest, education, or counseling, with that person."

In the *Hill* case, Leila Hill and other anti-abortion sidewalk counselors sought to have the statute struck down as unconstitutional, claiming that it violated their First Amendment rights. The American Center for Law and Justice argued this case with *amicus* support from the ACLU and People for the Ethical Treatment of Animals, organizations that ignored the content of the protester's message and focused instead on the direct threat to the free expression rights of protesters. The 6 to 3 split decision involved dissents by Justices Antonin Scalia, Anthony M. Kennedy, and Clarence Thomas. Kennedy complained that the decision "contradicts more than a half-century of well-established First Amendment principles." The *Hill* ruling was a monumental defeat for the rights of protesters.

Beyond supporting the freedom of speech rights of abortion protesters, movement attorneys have had crucial input in two cases that have delineated freedom of speech rights in recent years.

In 1992, in *R.A.V. v. City of Saint Paul*, the Supreme Court found unconstitutional a city ordinance forbidding the display on public or private property of objects, symbols, appellations, characterizations, or graffiti that one knows or has reason to know arouse "anger, alarm or resentment in others on the basis of race, color, creed, religion or gender." The case arose when the plaintiff was charged under the St. Paul Minnesota Bias-Motivated Crime Ordinance after allegedly burning a makeshift cross on the lawn of a black family.

The case pitted the movement's Center for Individual Rights and the ACLU with *amicus* briefs in favor of R.A.V. against the movement's Criminal Justice Legal Foundation and People for the American Way, which filed briefs in favor of the city's ordinance. The Supreme Court agreed that the ordinance facially violated the First Amendment because it applied only to words that insulted or provoked violence on the basis of race, color, creed, religion, or gender. In other words, the Supreme Court found that the ordinance was impermissibly content-based.

In 1995, in *Hurley v. Irish-American Gay, Lesbian and Bisexual Group of Boston*, the Supreme Court unanimously established the right of the St. Patrick's Day Parade organizers to control the political message of their own parade and exclude from their march any organization they believed would dilute their message. Funding was provided in part by the Alliance Defense Fund, and an *amicus* brief was filed by the California-based Individual Rights Foundation.

Freedom and the Boy Scouts

Perhaps the most significant recent decision protecting the right of all Americans to voluntary association and freedom of speech was the U.S. Supreme Court's 2000 ruling in *Boy Scouts of America v. Dale*. Overturning the New Jersey Supreme Court's split decision that the Scouts had violated the state's anti-discrimination law when they dismissed a gay Scout leader, the Court ruled that forcing the Boy Scouts to accept gays in leadership positions would violate the group's rights to freedom of association and free speech. Based in part on its 1995 decision in *Hurley*, the Court emphasized that it intended its ruling not as an endorsement of the Boy Scouts' position on homosexuality, but as a protection of the group's constitutional rights.

The *Dale* decision is a new bulwark for pluralism and the safeguarding of diverse viewpoints. It represents a monumental defeat for those who wish to use anti-discrimination laws to dictate membership in private voluntary associations—especially faith-based organizations. While this decision will protect the Ku Klux Klan's right to maintain its racist, sexist, and anti-Semitic profile, it also protects forward-thinking organizations' association rights. The case drew widespread *amicus* support from the Becket Fund for Religious Liberty, American Center for Law and Justice, American Civil Rights Union, Center for Individual Rights, Christian Legal Society, Pacific Legal Foundation, Southeastern Legal Foundation, Individual Rights Foundation, National Legal Foundation, and many others.

In contemporary America, an increasing number of citizens, judges, and government officials seem to believe that people—especially women, minorities, and other "historically disadvantaged" groups—have a right not to be offended and that this right supersedes the freedom of speech and association rights of others. As this belief gains wider acceptance, it threatens to have tragic consequences for the First Amendment to the Constitution.

The problem lies in a trend toward redefining civil rights and civil liberties to include protection from any conceivably discriminatory behavior and offensive speech. Historically, civil liberties protect individuals from government interference while civil rights confer some benefit. The redefinitions that have taken place have created an arena in which new "civil rights" conflict with traditional constitutional freedoms: freedom of speech, freedom of association, and freedom of religion.

"Hostile work environment" regulations, for example, threaten free expression in the workplace, but rarely with any identifiable consistency. The Center for Individual Rights led the fight to protect the First Amendment in *Aguilar v. Avis Rent-A-Car System, Inc.* In 1994, a group of Latino employees sued Avis Rent-a-Car for damages, alleging that the branch manager had created a hostile work environment by repeatedly calling Latino employees names and demeaning them on the basis of their race, national origin, and lack of English language skills.

The center's razor-sharp *amicus* brief, made all the more powerful because it brought together organizations from across the political and ideological spectrum including the National Writers Union, the Reason Foundation, and the Libertarian Law Council, argued that the court-ordered injunction forbidding "offensive epithets" in the workplace constituted unlawful prior restraint. Prior restraint is the most serious First Amendment violation—much worse than if the government punished someone *after* he has expressed himself—because it imposes censorship *before* the expression has taken place, so the unsuspecting public doesn't know that censorship has taken place.

In 2000, in a split decision, the California Supreme Court not only affirmed that the manager's speech had created a hostile work environment, but also upheld a prior restraint on future uses of racial epithets in the workplace. Dissenting Justice Janice Brown worried that this decision "would create the exception that swallowed the First Amendment," writing that "I can think of no circumstance in which this court has brushed aside such an important constitutional protection as the right to free speech on the basis of so little analysis or authority." When the U.S. Supreme Court declined to hear the case, Justice Clarence Thomas penned a vociferous dissent, arguing that this left unresolved the "troubling First Amendment issues" raised by the case.

The consequences of not reversing *Aguilar* and similar cases that extend and change the definition of "harassment" are abundantly clear in the arena of education. College and university administrators' attempts to create an inoffensive campus climate free from "discriminatory language" have led to "hostile environment"-motivated restrictions on academic freedom and freedom of speech.

Worse still, the selective enforcement of such speech codes entails the patronizing notion that some individuals, because of their color or gender, are simply too weak to study in an environment where an honest disagreement may offend them. The next generation is being taught that the proper response to speech one doesn't like is repression and censorship, not vigorous debate and moral witness.

Orwellian Campus Codes

During the late 1980s, students at the University of Michigan labored under a speech code that was representative of the sort found across the country. It was not called a speech code; they never are. Instead, it was called a "discrimination policy." It banned "verbal behavior" (an Orwellian euphemism for "speech") that "stigmatizes" or "victimizes" on the basis of race and a variety of other criteria so as to create a "demeaning environment." Examples of forbidden expressive conduct included making jokes or derogatory comments about someone's views or physical appearance and displaying a Confederate flag—all of which are constitutionally protected activities.

The case was litigated by the ACLU, which has subsequently cooperated with freedom-based movement organizations in speech code cases. Wes Wynne, a graduate student in biopsychology and a conservative activist, claimed that the university's speech code interfered with his right to discuss controversial theories of racial and sexual difference freely and openly in the classroom.

Doe v. University of Michigan was decided in 1989 by a Michigan district court. Upon examining prior applications of the policy, the court found that administrators had pursued complaints without considering whether the expression in question was protected under the First Amendment. Finding the policy overbroad and vague, the court ruled it unconstitutional on the grounds that it could not be enforced without violating the First Amendment rights of students and faculty. To its great shame, the University of Michigan had to be taught respect for academic freedom and free speech by a Michigan judge.

Two years later, the Center for Individual Rights, working with a Virginia ACLU attorney, sued George Mason University for using its speech code to punish a fraternity unfairly. In *Iota Xi Chapter of Sigma Chi Fraternity v. George Mason University*, members of Sigma Chi brought suit against the university after it sanctioned them for holding an "Ugly Woman Contest" in which several fraternity members dressed in drag. The contest drew 247 complaints for its "racist" and "sexist" content.

The case made its way up to the U.S. Court of Appeals for the Fourth Circuit, which in 1993 ruled that the First Amendment protected the students' skit because it fell under the category of "expressive entertainment." The court noted that "the First Amendment generally prevents government from proscribing ... expressive conduct because of disapproval of the ideas expressed."

Displaying an untenable double standard, the university had routinely permitted expressive conduct that offended students because of its racist and sexist content. The offended students in these instances were white and Christian, and their sensibilities had no standing whatsoever at George Mason. Freedom of speech, they were told, was an essential value in the university community.

Although speech that offends or hurts people's feelings is an inevitable result in a free society, the consequences of allowing government to try to police offensive expression would be disastrous. Further, it is even more dangerous to police such expression with a racial, ethnic, and sexual double standard. One undeniable reality of American history is that some of the greatest advances in our society—whether scientific, economic, religious, or political—could not have taken place without the right to freedom of speech.

Many who favor silencing "politically incorrect" campus views forget that there would have been no civil rights movement without freedom of speech. Unfortunately, many who delighted in—and benefited from—the Free Speech Movement of the 1960s are revealing themselves as generational charlatans now that they occupy positions of power within universities.

"The problems of bigotry and discrimination sought to be addressed here are real and truly corrosive of the educational environment," Senior U.S. District Court Judge Robert Warren wrote in 1991 when he struck down the University of Wisconsin speech code in *UWM Post, Inc. v. Board of Regents*. "But freedom of speech is almost absolute in our land...." In 1995, in *Dambrot v. Central Michigan University*, the university's speech code (embedded in its "discriminatory harassment" policy) was found to be unconstitutional after it was used to punish the head basketball coach for using racially derogatory terms.

In 2001, the Third Circuit unanimously determined in *Saxe v. State College Area School District* that the State College Area School District's anti-harassment speech code policy was unconstitutional after David Saxe, guardian to two students, filed suit alleging that the policy violated their First Amendment rights. The policy prohibited "verbal conduct" on matters of race, religion, gender, sexual orientation, and other characteristics if that conduct created a "hostile or offensive environment." Saxe claimed that the policy as written chilled his children's rights to religious expression, citing in particular his concern that it forbade them to express their Christian belief that homosexuality is a sin. The Foundation for Individual Rights in Education assisted the American Family Association with its winning brief.

The struggle against speech codes received an important boost in 2003 when the foundation, working with movement attorneys, brought about litigation against three codes in U.S. District Courts in *Bair v. Shippensburg University*, *Stevens v. Citrus College*, and *Roberts v. Haragan*.

In *Bair*, Pennsylvania's Shippensburg University banned speech that was "demeaning" and defined verbal harassment as conduct that "annoys" or "alarms" a person or group. The code also violated the right of private conscience by requiring that "every member of the community" mirror the official views of the university administration "in their attitudes and behaviors."

Walt Bair, the student plaintiff, testified that a university official ordered him to remove from his doors "messages or flyers that were hostile to Osama bin Laden and/or supportive of the American military effort in Afghanistan" following the terrorist attacks of September 11. Bair testified that the resident director of his dormitory informed him that such materials might be "offensive to other students and violated the Code of Conduct." A preliminary injunction issued by a judge became permanent when Shippensburg University agreed to strike the code.

The case involving California's Citrus College was settled within days of being filed when the college removed all unconstitutional language from its rule books. Texas Tech has responded to the Roberts suit, which is being handled by the Liberty Legal Institute and the Alliance Defense Fund, by altering its policies on its ironically named "free speech zones."

The Achilles' heel of the campus censors is that they cannot defend in public what they do to the individual rights of students and faculty. Sunlight truly is the best disinfectant.

Student Ignorance

Two surveys carried out in 2003 and funded by the John M. Templeton Foundation revealed that college and university students are woefully ignorant about freedom of speech and freedom of religion. One out of every four undergraduates is unable to mention any freedoms protected by the First Amendment, and only 30 percent of them answered correctly that freedom of religion is a right guaranteed by the First Amendment to the U.S. Constitution.[2]

Administrators who govern student life on campus fared no better. Only 21 percent of the interviewed administrators named the very first right guaranteed by the Bill of Rights—freedom of religion—when asked to name any First Amendment right, and a full 11 percent admitted that they did not know any of the specific rights guaranteed by the First Amendment.

Because college and university administrators and students largely fail to understand the nature of freedom of speech, it is not surprising that students across the nation have blithely endured many restrictions and double standards that violate their essential freedoms. Most conservative and religious students (especially Christian students) choose to engage in self-censorship because the intellectual climate on campus is so intolerant of their positions that they fear they will be ostracized and treated as moral pariahs simply for having a different point of view.

Literally hundreds of students are persecuted every year for holding views that are "offensive." Many of these students fatalistically accept their situation and submit to university censorship. Others, lacking a legal basis for a claim, are underserved by friends of liberty.

In the past four years, however, new and existing organizations have begun to advocate free speech on campus more strenuously through grassroots organizations and public exposure. Such activities are beginning to shift the public agenda as more and more people understand the importance of addressing universities' illiberal policies.

It is important to mention the contributions made by organizations such as the National Association of Scholars, the Federalist Society, the Intercollegiate Studies Institute, Students for Academic Freedom, the Leadership Institute, the Independent Women's Forum, and the American Council of Trustees and Alumni to raising awareness about these issues. Judges do not rule in a vacuum; the cultural climate is an essential component in the struggle for liberty.

The past 30 years of legal history have seen movement attorneys involved in many of the crucial cases concerning freedom of speech. Currently, movement attorneys display the same vigor and passion for protecting fundamental rights as they ponder the December 2003 Supreme Court ruling in favor of the existing campaign finance legislation.

The future of freedom of speech, whether on campus, in the streets, or in electoral politics, will continue to depend in large part on the vital work performed by the dedicated organizations and attorneys affiliated with the freedom-based public interest law movement.

---

[1] A notable exception is cases involving the freedom of speech rights of Jehovah's Witnesses.

[2] The surveys were carried out by the Center for Survey Research and Analysis at the University of Connecticut and were commissioned by the Foundation for Individual Rights in Education.

CHAPTER 8

Protecting Workers' Rights

David Kendrick

Th_he right to join a labor union and, conversely, the right *not*
to join a union or to pay dues against one's will should be
a fundamental freedom of the workplace. The fight for
this right by public interest legal groups began in 1968 with the
founding of the National Right to Work Legal Defense Foundation but its roots go back to the early 1950s and the emergence of
the extraordinary leadership of Reed Larson.

Larson's commitment to the cause of voluntary unionism
intensified in 1954 at the bedside of Deering Crowe, a taxi driver
who chose to work during a taxi strike in Wichita, Kansas. Larson was on "temporary leave" from his job at the Coleman Company in order to head a group called Kansans for the Right to
Work. The strike had been instigated by national Teamsters boss
Dave Beck, who demanded that all Wichita taxi drivers be forced
to join the union.

As part of a campaign of intimidation, Crowe was called to a
fictitious address. Union goons beat him with chains and then left
him with the words, "This will teach you to be a scab." Two days
earlier, doctors had scheduled an operation to remove a malig-

nant tumor from Crowe's face, but the brutal attack forced doctors to delay the operation until it was too late to remove the cancer completely. Crowe died in November 1954, but not before the Larson interview. A half-century later, this encounter remains "painfully vivid" in Larson's mind. Deering Crowe "stands out" to Larson "as a disfigured monument to the brutal tactics of Big Labor."[1]

Larson moved to Washington, D.C., to lead the National Right to Work Committee, a small but determined organization upholding right-to-work laws, which prohibit the forcing of workers to join a union as a condition of employment. By the end of 1966, the group had scored a major and improbable victory.

Repeal of the Taft–Hartley Act's Section 14(b), which allows states to adopt right-to-work laws, seemed all but assured in the wake of President Lyndon Johnson's 1964 landslide election and the Democrats' sweep of Congress, but an intensive public affairs campaign during which almost every daily newspaper in America editorialized against repeal, plus a filibuster led by Senate minority Leader Everett Dirksen (R–IL), pushed the Democrats into abandoning their repeal effort. The committee successfully harnessed public sentiment, confirmed by years of polling, that an overwhelming majority of Americans believed that no one should be forced to join a union as a condition of employment.

By 1968, the committee had agreed to support several individuals in legal actions who were victims of compulsory unionism. That year, the committee's board of directors approved Larson's request for a separate organization to focus on the courts, while the committee would focus its efforts entirely on the legislative arena. The National Right to Work Legal Defense Foundation was established as a nonprofit charitable organization, with two equally important objectives: enforce employees' existing legal rights against forced unionism abuses and win new legal precedents expanding those rights and protections.

The reasons for establishing the foundation were compelling. Larson saw how effectively liberal legal aid groups like the NAACP Legal Defense and Education Fund and the American Civil Liberties Union had shaped public policy by assisting individual clients. These were "charitable" groups, fueled by tax-deductible dollars, whose arguments fell on increasingly sympathetic ears in the courts, including the Supreme Court. Led by Chief Justice Earl Warren, the high court crafted ruling after ruling that affected public policy as surely as congressional legislation did.

Larson also saw individual employees calling the committee regularly because they had nowhere else to turn. The National Labor Relations Act sanctioned the forcing of employees to pay union dues as a condition of employment, but what really brought workplace tyranny to life were contracts in which the employer submitted to union demands to fire non-payers. Even if workers could afford them, most labor law specialists worked for the union or management, not the employee. The desperate situation of workers was cited by law professor and eventual Watergate prosecutor Archibald Cox. "Individual workers who sue union officials run enormous risks," Cox said, "for there are many ways, legal as well as illegal, by which entrenched union officials can 'take care of' recalcitrant members."[2]

For three years, the National Right to Work Legal Defense Foundation retained outside legal counsel to handle the requests for assistance. But by 1971, Larson realized that its litigation program would be more efficient and effective in the hands of in-house legal staff. That year, the foundation hired Raymond LaJeunesse as its first staff attorney. Today LaJeunesse serves as the foundation's vice president and legal director, succeeding Rex H. Reed, who retired in 2001.

That same year, the foundation argued its first case before the U.S. Supreme Court, albeit with disappointing results. In *Street, Electric Railway & Motor Coach Employees v. Lockridge*, the

Court dealt workers a setback, granting the National Labor Relations Board exclusive jurisdiction over the claims of employees discharged under forced-membership contracts. The ruling largely preempted the authority of state courts to judge such claims except under right-to-work laws.

Despite this disappointment, however, the foundation's model for public interest litigation caught the attention of other conservatives. In California, the Chamber of Commerce, working with William French Smith, Ronald Reagan's personal attorney, investigated the possibility of setting up a nonprofit law firm to fight government intrusion on property rights. After a careful study of the foundation and its operations, the Pacific Legal Foundation was founded with J. Simon Fluor at its helm.

"Sinful and Tyrannical"

The situation in the courts worsened in 1973 when the U.S. Court of Appeals for the Tenth Circuit ruled, in *Reid v. United Auto Workers*, that employees forced to pay for the United Auto Workers political activity had to trust in the UAW's own rebate procedure to get refunds of forced dues spent on politics. The Tenth Circuit had empowered the fox to guard the chicken coop. Union officials could prevent judicial inquiry into their spending practices simply by setting up phony rebate procedures. Despite the setback in *Reid*, foundation attorneys clung stubbornly to the constitutional principle, perfectly expressed by Thomas Jefferson, that "to compel a man to furnish contributions of money for the propagation of opinions which he disbelieves is sinful and tyrannical."

In 1977, the high court finally accepted this argument. In *Abood v. Detroit Board of Education*, a six-member majority upheld local school boards' practice of requiring the payment of union fees as a condition of employment. But the Court—specifically citing Jefferson's principle—also held unanimously that, while forced payments to the union did not violate the First Amendment's guarantee of free speech, this was true *only* "insofar as the service charges are applied to collective-bargaining, contract administration, and grievance-adjustment purposes." The entire Court agreed that "a union cannot constitutionally spend [objectors'] funds for the expression of political views, on behalf of political candidates, or toward the advancement of other ideological causes not germane to its duties as collective-bargaining representative."

As a practical matter, however, workers found themselves with few new protections. Most union officials completely ignored the Supreme Court's clear intent in *Abood* that no one should be forced to pay for political causes with which they disagreed. Instead, they contrived elaborate, time-consuming procedures for non-members to request a refund of those dues spent on non-bargaining activities. One arrogant public-sector union, a Communication Workers local in New Jersey, decreed that the refundable amount of forced-dues payers' fees was just 1 cent and insisted that the refund request be sent to the union by certified mail.

Foundation attorneys sought to capitalize on the principle established in the *Abood* case and commenced another challenge to big labor's forced-dues regime, filing a class-action suit on behalf of Howard Ellis and more than 200 Western Airlines employees who objected to being forced to support the political machine of the Brotherhood of Railway, Airline and Steamship Clerks. The plaintiffs also protested being forced to rely on the union's rebate procedure, which they likened to a "kangaroo court."

Union officials sought dismissal of the suit on the basis of the 1973 *Reid* decision, in which the Tenth Circuit had upheld the UAW's internal procedures. But the Railway Labor Act, under which transportation employees like Ellis were covered, imposes even more government control of that labor market than the National Labor Relations Act, under which *Reid* was brought. Thus, the clerks' union violation of the workers' rights was more obvious, and more troubling.

Foundation attorneys achieved a breakthrough when U.S. District Judge Leland Nielsen ruled that the union's rebate procedure improperly provided refunds only for certain political activities rather than for all union activities unrelated to collective bargaining. The court held that the union had spent compulsory fees for a variety of illegal purposes, such as entertainment for union bosses, membership recruitment, union organizing efforts in other companies, union propaganda, convention expenses, and charitable contributions, as well as union political lobbying and contributions.

In addition to rejecting the union's sham rebate procedure, Judge Nielsen also ruled that the individual employees objecting to the union's illegal spending practices were entitled to bring a class-action suit for all other Western Airlines employees in a similar situation. For the first time, a concept previously the exclusive territory of the Left—shaping public policy through litigation—had been opened to employees, to use against union spending abuses.

The union appealed to the Ninth Circuit Court of Appeals, which reversed Nielsen's ruling, and foundation attorneys, based on the strength of the district court's opinion and a strong dissenting opinion at the appellate level, then appealed to the Supreme Court. In April 1984, the high court unanimously upheld Nielsen's decision, ruling that "the union cannot be allowed to commit dissenters' funds to improper uses—even temporarily." In other words, union officials could not derive the benefit of forced dues spent on politics and then refund to objecting employees what never should have been seized in the first place.

After *Ellis v. Brotherhood of Railway Clerks*, regrettably, several lower court cases were decided against employee plaintiffs because the Supreme Court had not defined the procedural, due process rights of employees whose constitutional rights were violated. Two years later, however, the foundation was to win another Supreme Court victory on that particular issue.

Foundation attorneys represented a group of public school teachers, led by Annie Lee Hudson, in a suit against the Chicago Teachers Union, challenging the union's scheme for determining the amount of the compulsory "agency fee" the teachers could be required to pay. After losing at the district court, the attorneys won at the Seventh Circuit Court of Appeals and then defended Hudson and her fellow teachers before the Supreme Court.

In March 1986, the high court ruled 9 to 0 that the First Amendment requires that government employers and public-sector unions must provide dissident public employees with due process safeguards in the determination of the percentage of dues they could be required to pay.

As a result of the foundation's victory in *Chicago Teachers Union v. Hudson*, officials of public employee unions must notify employees of the forced-dues deductions before they begin. They must also submit to an independent audit to justify the percentage of membership dues they claim to be bargaining-related. Employees who choose to challenge that determination are entitled to a prompt, impartial review and to have any "amounts reasonably in dispute" placed in escrow pending the outcome of litigation.

In addition, because the Court had earlier ruled that its interpretations of the Constitution applied to the Railway Labor Act, the due process safeguards of the *Hudson* ruling also apply to those employees covered by the earlier *Ellis* case.

Rights and Union Politics

Attorneys for the National Right to Work Legal Defense Foundation had won for unionized employees in government, airlines, and railroads the right not to pay for union politics and other non-bargaining activities. Whether this right applied to the majority of American workers—the more than 44 million covered by the National Labor Relations Act—remained an open question. It was a question that Maryland telephone lineman Harry Beck was raising in the federal courts with the assistance of foundation attorneys.

Beck had been a shop steward with the Communications Workers of America until he resigned from the union over its 1968 political endorsements and ceased paying any dues to the union. Then, in 1974, Bell Telephone agreed to an "agency shop" clause in its new contract with the union as part of a strike settlement. Suddenly, Beck found himself being forced to pay a non-member's "agency fee" that was equivalent to full membership dues. Knowing firsthand how those dues and fees would go to support political candidates and causes with which he disagreed, Beck sought the assistance of the National Right to Work Legal Defense Foundation. Its attorneys took up his fight, filing suit against the union in 1976.

Three years later, U.S. District Judge C. Stanley Blair found it unconstitutional for private-sector unions to collect or spend compulsory fees for any purpose other than collective bargaining, contract administration, or grievance processing. Blair then appointed a special master to determine how much of Beck's forced dues the union had spent on non-bargaining purposes. In 1981, the special master concluded that the union had only proven that 21 percent of Beck's payments to the union was related to collective bargaining.

Recognizing the momentous precedent Judge Blair's ruling could set, the AFL–CIO joined the communications workers' union in appealing to the U.S. Court of Appeals for the Fourth Circuit. When they did not like the 2 to 1 ruling of the special panel that heard their appeal, the union attorneys demanded and got a rehearing before all ten judges in the Fourth Circuit. The result was a 6 to 4 decision upholding Beck and his fellow plaintiffs. The Supreme Court agreed to hear the union's appeal in 1987.

In June 1988, the high court decided the case in Beck's favor. Writing for a 5 to 3 majority (with one justice abstaining), Justice William Brennan wrote that Congress intended the substantially "identical" authorizations of compulsory unionism in the National Labor Relations Act and the Railway Labor Act "to have the same meaning." The Court had already ruled four years earlier in *Ellis* that employees covered under the Railway Labor Act could not be forced to pay for non-bargaining activities. Likewise, Brennan wrote, the National Labor Relations Act "authorizes the exaction of only those fees and dues necessary to 'performing the duties of an exclusive representative of the employees in dealing with the employer on labor-management issues.'"

Twenty years after its founding, the foundation had won for all employees nationwide the right to stop the use of forced dues for political causes and candidates they had no wish to support. Establishing legal precedents, however, is one thing. Enforcing them is another. In the years since *Communication Workers of America v. Beck*, the National Right to Work Legal Defense Foundation has been forced to return to the courts time and time again in defense of the principle affirmed in *Beck*.

In 1991, in *Lehnert v. Ferris Faculty Association*, the Supreme Court specifically disallowed the following activities to be charged to the objecting teachers: litigation unrelated to the employees' bargaining unit, lobbying unrelated to ratification of or fiscal appropriations for their bargaining agreement, public relations activities, and illegal strikes.

In May 1998, foundation attorneys beat back another attempt by union officials to keep employees from finding out how much the union spends on politics and other non-bargaining activities. For years, union officials had attempted to force workers who object to paying for union politics into union-run "arbitration" hearings. That the "arbitrator" is hand-picked and paid by the union raises serious questions about the impartiality of these decision-makers. Employees forced into such hearings are also hamstrung by their inability to examine the union's financial records regarding where their membership dues are spent.

In April 1997, foundation attorneys persuaded the U.S. Court of Appeals for the District of Columbia that union officials should not be allowed to prevent workers from filing suit to obtain full discovery of the union's records. Attorneys for the Air Line Pilots Association appealed to the U.S. Supreme Court. In May 1998, in *Air Line Pilots Association v. Miller*, the Court agreed with foundation attorneys that employees who oppose union officials' spending of their forced dues have the right to go directly to federal court to subpoena union books and records and depose union officials about their activities.

Later in 1998, in *Marquez v. Screen Actors Guild*, the Court ruled for the first time that union officials are obligated to inform employees of their right under *Beck* not to pay for non-bargaining activities. In their unanimous decision reaffirming *Beck*, the high court also set that precedent on firmer ground than the closer 5 to 3 decision in 1988.

Financial Impact

While the National Right to Work Legal Defense Foundation has altered the legal landscape for employee protections against compulsory unionism, its class-action victories have had a more immediate impact on organized labor—in the wallet. Since 1988, for example, foundation attorneys represented Pennsylvania state employees in federal court in *Hohe v. Casey*. Building on previous Supreme Court victories in *Abood*, *Hudson*, and *Lehnert*, foundation attorneys negotiated a settlement in early 1995 with the American Federation of State, County and Municipal Employees, AFL–CIO. In the settlement, officials from the government workers' union agreed to refund, with interest, over $8 million to more than 57,000 Pennsylvania state employees.

Since its founding in 1968, the foundation has provided free legal aid to about 20,000 individual workers and has assisted more than 368,000 employees through class actions while winning or settling favorably nearly 2,000 cases in federal and state courts and administrative agencies.

After nearly 50 years of service to the right-to-work cause, Reed Larson stepped down as president of the foundation and the

National Right to Work Committee in April 2003, handing the reins of the movement over to Mark Mix, who had worked with Larson for 17 years. Mix credits Larson's leadership with helping to keep the right-to-work movement's message consistent and principled while staying focused on the long term. "National Right to Work," says Mix, "has always maintained that the ultimate solution to Big Labor abuses is the abolition of forced union membership, forced-dues payment, and forced union 'representation' as conditions of employment."[3]

The primary reason *Beck* has not been enforced by federal agencies has been the alliance of union bosses and political figures. One of President Clinton's first acts in office, for example, was to repeal an executive order of the first President Bush that required notices in the workplaces of federal contractors informing unionized employees of their *Beck* rights. It was not long before Clinton was trading golf club gifts with Arthur Coia, president of the Laborers International Union of North America (LIUNA), who became one of Clinton's biggest supporters.

On the same day in 1994 that Clinton wrote a thank-you letter to Coia for his new driver, the Department of Justice informed the union that it was prepared to file a federal racketeering suit against it. The department alleged in a draft complaint that LIUNA was "controlled and/or substantially influenced by organized crime." LIUNA officials hired the same law firm that was representing the Clintons in the Whitewater real estate scandal, and the Justice Department dropped the suit in 1995. Instead, it allowed the union to "reform itself."

The next year, it was discovered that a number of liberal and Democrat-affiliated groups had funneled contributions to Teamster President Ron Carey's re-election campaign in exchange for the Teamsters' financial support of the Clinton–Gore re-election campaign. The contributions to Carey were barred by federal law, which prohibited any employers from contributing funds to union elections.

Confronting the Union–Political Boss Axis

Out of a desire to confront union bosses and their political patrons directly on the corruption issue, the National Legal and Policy Center in late 1997 launched the Organized Labor Accountability Project. The center was founded in 1991 by Ken Boehm and Peter Flaherty to promote ethics in public life through litigation, research, and public education. It is the only national clearinghouse on union corruption, publishing the *Union Corruption Update* newsletter every two weeks. The center exposes and attacks union corruption in the "court of public opinion" and seeks to influence policymakers in the executive and legislative branches of the federal government.

Although there was no hope in 2000 that the Clinton administration would pursue reforms to combat corruption, the National Legal and Policy Center helped to lay the groundwork for future reforms. Staff member Michael Nelson, then a student at George Mason University School of Law, wrote a law review article titled "Slowing Union Corruption: Reforming the Landrum–Griffin Act to Better Combat Union Embezzlement." Passed in 1959 and known officially as the Labor-Management Reporting and Disclosure Act, Landrum–Griffin made it a federal crime to embezzle union member dues and gave union members certain rights to act as a check on the power of union bosses, including the right to sue for breaches of fiduciary duty and to access financial information about their unions. Nelson proposed eight changes to make Landrum–Griffin more effective in deterring and punishing union embezzlement.

Two years later, George W. Bush was President and Elaine Chao was Secretary of Labor. In May 2002, the center submitted a 37-page petition to Chao based on Nelson's article. It proposed an overhaul of the LM-2 financial disclosure forms that the nation's wealthiest unions must file with the Department of Labor. Seven months later, the department did just that, proposing to require that union officials report how much they spend on politics and lobbying, as well as account for their own paid time spent on such activities.

One of the major roadblocks to enforcement of *Beck* has been the lack of obligation for union officials to report any political expenditures beyond direct contributions to candidates. Left undisclosed are the costs of phone banks, door-to-door canvasses, voter-turnout drives, and other "in-kind" activities. Obligating union officials who represent private-sector employees to report those expenses will finally give employees accurate information about how much of their forced dues they can recover by asserting their *Beck* rights.

These new LM-2 forms, due to legal actions, are scheduled to go into effect in July 2004, and although the new disclosure rules have been criticized for not going far enough, they are the first tightening of disclosure requirements in 40 years. Secretary Chao represents a break with the past. In both Democratic and Republican administrations, labor secretaries have been captives, to a lesser or greater extent, of the union bosses.

Another challenge to the alliance of union bosses and political figures is coming from the Landmark Legal Foundation. Established in 1976, Landmark's long record of accomplishments—from combating judicial taxation and racial quotas in the Kansas City, Missouri, desegregation litigation to defending economic liberty and private property rights, as well as its path-breaking defense of the Milwaukee Parental Choice Plan—make it one of the nation's most effective and successful conservative legal advocacy groups.

In June 2000, Landmark President Mark Levin took aim at the National Education Association. Landmark filed formal complaints with the Internal Revenue Service and the Federal Election Commission against the NEA for failing to comply fully with federal tax and campaign laws. Federal law requires the NEA to pay taxes on any funds used to influence candidate elections, but its previous tax returns reported no political expenditures.

Landmark charged that at least since 1994—the year Landmark began tracking the union's political expenditures—the NEA spent tens of millions of dollars derived from its members' tax-exempt dues payments on unreported political expenditures and activities. In November 2003, NEA President Reg Weaver revealed that the IRS informed the teachers union in September that it would soon conduct an audit of its finances.

In Washington state, the Evergreen Freedom Foundation, headed by Bob Williams, is doing battle with the Washington Education Association and other unions. Since 1996, through litigation and public relations, the foundation has fought successfully to keep the union from suppressing teachers' right to free speech.

Washington was the first state to enact a law requiring unions to obtain annual written permission from workers before using their payroll deductions for politics. The law was passed by voter initiative in 1992, with 72 percent support. After it was adopted, more than 85 percent of teachers chose not to support the union's politics.

These advances by public interest legal groups are interim steps toward a larger goal. As Harry Beck puts it, "until Congress repeals or the high court overturns the federal sanction of compulsory dues, workers will not have their full freedoms."

---

[1] *National Right to Work Newsletter*, National Right to Work Committee, June 2003, special insert, p. 3.

[2] *Michigan Law Review*, Vol. 58 (1960), p. 853.

[3] *Foundation Action*, National Right to Work Legal Defense Foundation, May–June 2003, p. 3.

CHAPTER 9

Following the Money

Mark R. Levin

In *The Right Stuff*, his book about the early days of the space program, Tom Wolfe recounts an exchange between two men involved in America's effort to break the sound barrier in 1947. One of the men asked the other, a test pilot, "What makes these supersonic planes go? What makes them fly?" The pilot answered that the aerodynamics alone would take hours to explain. "Wrong," the man corrected him. "Money makes these planes fly. No Bucks, no Buck Rogers."

It is much the same in the public interest law movement. Without hundreds of millions of dollars in annual grants from the nation's richest foundations, the liberal legal activists who have dominated the public policy landscape for much of the past several decades would be little more than shadows in the wilderness, and their objectives of ever-expanding government control over private industry and the private lives of America's citizens would be nothing more than unrealistic, unrealizable pipe dreams.

This phenomenon is ironic since most of the foundations that fund the activities of liberal groups were made possible by the generosity of individuals who never intended for their fortunes to be used to undermine the very economic system and social institutions that fostered their entrepreneurial success. Many foundations that were started by entrepreneurs who valued the free market and supported a limited role for government have been transformed into virtual ATMs for liberal causes.

While it is true that a few of the principal sources of money for liberal activists were founded by business leaders with a liberal ideological bent (the Hewlett and the Packard foundations, to name two), many others have mutated toward left-leaning social agendas as the founding generation stepped away or died and the organizations' leadership was assumed by other family members (wives, children, grandchildren, etc.) or, in some cases, unrelated professional managers in the nonprofit community.

Patterns of Foundation Grant-Making

Moreover, a number of America's great foundations were started to fulfill limited, essentially apolitical social purposes (support for a local community, promoting child welfare, advancing the arts, etc.), but as these organizations have grown financially, new generations of managers have used the enhanced assets to fund program areas and projects that have little or no connection to the roots of the foundation (the Kellogg and Starr foundations are examples of this sort of evolution). These nonprofit professionals have inculcated their own cultural agendas into the foundations' institutional priorities. The addition of individuals with predetermined political and/or social agendas to the boards of many foundations has also hastened this change.

In truth, six of America's top ten grant-making foundations give tens of millions of dollars each year to liberal groups like the American Civil Liberties Union, NAACP Legal Defense and Education Fund, Natural Resources Defense Council, Environmental Defense Fund, National Organization for Women, World Wildlife Fund, and a host of other organizations. The large grant-making foundations have underwritten litigation to defeat school vouchers, promote gay rights, impose politically correct curricula in public schools, and otherwise write the liberal activist social agenda into the law of the land. Moreover, groups like People for the American Way receive millions from the large foundations to conduct broad-based public education campaigns against conservative federal judges and nominees to cabinet positions, to advance public acceptance of liberal causes, and to silence public commentary by conservatives.

Foundations that focus their philanthropy on identifiably conservative objectives are significantly smaller than their liberal counterparts, and the support offered by those foundations to conservative public advocacy groups is a fraction of that offered to liberal groups. Groups like my own Landmark Legal Foundation are forced by necessity to counter the actions of the liberal activists and their foundation funders with far fewer human and institutional resources and far less money than are available to our opponents. This "David and Goliath" disparity of resources alone makes the victories our movement has achieved in the Clarence Thomas nomination, the Milwaukee and Cleveland school voucher cases, the Wilkinsburg, Pennsylvania, privatization case, the gross abuse of the judicial process in the 2000 presidential election, and the nomination of Attorney General John Ashcroft—to name just a few examples—all the more impressive.

The grant-making patterns exhibited by some of America's leading foundations illustrate the disparity in the resources available to liberal and conservative public interest groups. (The number in parentheses after each foundation's name indicates the foundation's place in the most recent list of top 100 U.S. foundations by asset size, as published by the Foundation Center. The remaining foundations on the list do not fund liberal organizations in any substantial or programmatic fashion.)

Ford Foundation (3)

The Ford Foundation declares that its mission is to serve as "a resource for innovative people and institutions worldwide. Our goals are to: Strengthen democratic values, reduce poverty and injustice, promote international cooperation and advance human achievement."[1]

Started in 1936, the foundation began with gifts of Ford Motor Company stock from Henry and Edsel Ford. Initially a local philanthropic organization in Michigan, it later was transformed into a national group that supports primarily liberal organizations and/or causes. The foundation is now separate from the Ford Motor Company, and there are no members of the Ford family or officers of the company on the foundation's board of directors. (However, the president and CEO of the World Wildlife Fund is on the board of trustees, along with a former CEO of Xerox, the chairman and CEO of Alcoa, the general counsel of Coca-Cola, and other industry and nonprofit leaders.)

Today, the foundation's holdings are diversified, and it no longer owns Ford Motor Company stock. Throughout its life, the Ford Foundation has given away more than $12 billion in grants, project funds, and loans.[2] It now has $9.1 billion in assets and is America's third largest foundation.[3]

Among the many liberal groups that the Ford Foundation supports are the following:[4]

- American Civil Liberties Union
- American Civil Liberties Union Foundation
- Environmental Law Institute
- Friends of the Earth
- Mexican American Legal Defense and Educational Fund
- NAACP Legal Defense and Education Fund
- National Council of La Raza
- National Organization for Women

- National Wildlife Federation
- Nature Conservancy
- Puerto Rican Legal Defense and Education Fund
- World Resources Institute
- World Wildlife Fund

David and Lucille Packard Foundation (6)

The David and Lucille Packard Foundation was created in 1964 by one of the co-founders of the Hewlett–Packard Company and his wife, Lucille Salter Packard. Much of David Packard's estate was left to the foundation after his death in 1996.[5] As of December 2002, the foundation had assets totaling nearly $4.9 billion, most of which consisted of 194 million shares of Hewlett–Packard Company stock. The foundation made $167.7 million in grants in 2002.[6]

Today, the foundation is run by a board of trustees that includes several Packard family members and other nonprofit and private-sector leaders. Grants are centered around four major goals: "to ensure opportunities for all children to reach their potential, to protect reproductive rights and stabilize world population, to conserve and restore the earth's natural systems and to encourage the creative pursuit of science."[7] Its major program areas are conservation and science, population, children, families and communities, and special opportunities and capacity building.[8] In addition to its grant-making operations, one of the foundation's major operations is the Monterey Bay Aquarium Research Institute in Moss Landing, California.

Among the liberal organizations that receive grants from the David and Lucille Packard Foundation are the following:[9]

- American Civil Liberties Union Foundation of Northern California
- Center for Policy Alternatives
- Environmental Defense Fund
- International Planned Parenthood Federation

- Medical Students for Choice
- National Abortion and Reproductive Rights Action League Foundation
- Natural Resources Defense Council
- Population Council
- Strategies for the Global Environment
- World Wildlife Fund

William and Flora Hewlett Foundation (7)

The William and Flora Hewlett Foundation has been making grants since its inception in 1966. It was founded by William Hewlett, one of the co-founders of the Hewlett–Packard Company; his wife, Flora Lamson Hewlett; and their eldest son, Walter B. Hewlett. The foundation is the seventh largest in the United States, with assets of more than $5 billion,[10] and expected to distribute $254,320,000 to 707 organizations in 2003.[11]

The Hewlett Foundation describes itself as "concerned primarily with solving social and environmental problems."[12] Major areas of interest are conflict resolution, education, the environment, performing arts, population issues, and U.S.–Latin American relations. It also has "initiatives supporting neighborhood improvement, philanthropy, and global affairs," the second of which includes "improving the quantity and quality of ... information about the objectives and performance of nonprofit organizations, including foundations."[13]

The following are some of the organizations supported by the William and Flora Hewlett Foundation:[14]

- Environmental Defense Fund
- Mexican American Legal Defense and Educational Fund
- Natural Resources Defense Council
- Sierra Club
- World Wildlife Fund
- Zero Population Growth

W. K. Kellogg Foundation (8)

Will Keith Kellogg, the inventor of the corn flake, created the W. K. Kellogg Foundation in 1930 as the W. K. Kellogg Child Welfare Foundation after he had served as a delegate to a White House conference on child welfare and protection. The foundation's name was changed a few months later when Kellogg broadened the organization's scope. While the foundation focuses on the Greater Battle Creek, Michigan, area where it is headquartered, it makes grants to charities in the United States, Latin America, the Caribbean, and the nations of Botswana, Lesotho, Mozambique, South Africa, Swaziland, and Zimbabwe in southern Africa.

Two principal Kellogg Foundation grant-making areas are community-based health care improvement programs and rural development, in the latter case with an emphasis on "environmentally sensitive, sustainable long-term, and socially responsible" food-related business systems.[15] In its youth and education programs, it supports "a holistic, child-centered approach" to the "preschool through college continuum—ages 0-24."[16] The foundation also supports programs geared toward enhancing philanthropy by encouraging a broader base of financial support for charities.

Since Kellogg's death in 1951, the foundation has undergone a series of changes in philosophy and scope that has made it one of the most generous supporters of liberal causes and organizations in America, all under the rubric of its original focus on young people. In the 1950s and 1960s, the foundation focused on building up the community college movement and on health care education. In the 1970s, it moved toward greater support for programs for minorities. In the 1980s, it added a focus on southern Africa and created a more formalized approach to its core areas of support.

In 2003, the W. K. Kellogg Foundation approved 760 grants totaling $221,522,283.[17] The foundation had $5,530,494,099 in total assets for the same year.[18] Among the many liberal organizations that the Kellogg Foundation supports are the following:[19]

- Alternative Energy Resources Organization
- American Civil Liberties Union
- Environmental Defense Fund
- Mexican American Legal Defense and Educational Fund
- National Council of La Raza
- Nature Conservancy
- World Wildlife Fund

Starr Foundation (9)

Cornelius Vander Starr, who started what is now the American International Group insurance conglomerate, created the Starr Foundation in 1955 as the principal vehicle for his personal philanthropy. When he died in 1968 at the age of 76, he left his estate to the foundation. The Starr Foundation now has assets totaling nearly $4.8 billion and gave out $245,469,098 in grants in 2001.[20] The bulk of its grants go to support scholarships and scholarship programs in the U.S. and around the world.

Other areas of concentration include medicine and health care, including medical research, capital grants for hospitals, and delivery services for underserved areas around New York City and overseas, and support for emergency food programs, literacy programs, and projects that provide housing for the underprivileged in and around New York City, where the foundation is headquartered. The foundation also funds museums and community-based programs that provide cultural services to the elderly.

Liberal organizations that receive funding from the Starr Foundation include the following:[21]

- Natural Resources Defense Council
- Nature Conservancy
- Planned Parenthood—New York, NY

• Population Council

It should also be noted, however, that the Starr Foundation exhibits a curious dichotomy in the groups it supports. In addition to offering substantial financial backing to many of the most strident liberal nonprofits, the foundation also provides grants to traditionally conservative or libertarian groups like The Heritage Foundation, the Manhattan Institute, the Competitive Enterprise Institute, and the Hoover Institution.

John D. and Catherine T. MacArthur Foundation (10)

In 1935, John D. MacArthur purchased the Bankers Life and Casualty Company of Chicago with $2,500 he borrowed. When he died in 1978, the company was worth more than $1 billion. In addition to Bankers Life, MacArthur at one point or another owned more than 100,000 acres of land, largely in Palm Beach and Sarasota, Florida, as well as numerous development companies, paper and pulp companies, radio and television stations, banks, and 12 other insurance companies.

At the time of his death in 1978, John D. MacArthur was the third richest man in America. His wife Catherine was intimately involved in the operation of his companies and, later, in the running of the John D. and Catherine T. MacArthur Foundation.

The MacArthur Foundation now has assets of nearly $4 billion and made 657 grants in 2002 totaling $225.9 million, including the well-known MacArthur Fellowships.[22] The MacArthur Fellows Program awards five-year unrestricted fellowships to individuals across all ages and fields who show exceptional merit and the promise of continued creative work. The program is available only to U.S. citizens or residents of the United States.

The foundation's four major program areas include Global Security and Sustainability, which supports efforts to promote peace and security, conservation and sustainable development, population and reproductive health, human rights, and the consequences of globalization, primarily in Russia, Nigeria, Mexico, and India; Human and Community Development, which focuses on community development, regional policy, affordable housing, the preservation of rental housing, and systemic reform in education, juvenile justice, and mental health in the United States; a General Program of support to public interest media, including the production of independent documentaries, and large arts and cultural organizations in the Chicago, Illinois, area where the foundation is headquartered; and Program-Related Investments, which makes low-cost loans and investments in housing, community facilities, and affordable banking services for low-income individuals.

Among the liberal recipients of MacArthur Foundation grants are the following:[23]

- Alliance for Justice
- EarthJustice Legal Defense Fund
- Environmental Defense Fund
- Friends of the Earth
- Mexican American Legal Defense and Educational Fund
- National Council of La Raza
- National Wildlife Federation
- Natural Resources Defense Council
- Nature Conservancy
- Population Action International
- Sierra Club
- Union of Concerned Scientists
- World Wildlife Fund

How the Left Uses the Money

It is striking, when reviewing the largesse of the large foundations, to see how narrowly focused and closed-minded those organizations are. For all the rhetoric offered by these foundations about such objectives as diversity, inclusion, innovation, and real-world impact, much of their grant-making revolves around empty platitudes and self-serving generalities that often have little relation to the realities of the environments in which they operate.

The other half of the equation is, of course, the organizations that actually advance the cause through litigation, regulatory initiatives, and public advocacy—the groups in the left-wing trenches that receive the money from the large grant-making foundations: organizations like the NAACP Legal Defense and Education Fund, American Civil Liberties Union, Alliance for Justice, People for the American Way, and, in the environmental arena, the Environmental Defense Fund, Natural Resources Defense Council, Sierra Club, and Union of Concerned Scientists, in addition to a host of other issue- and area-specific nonprofit organizations.

These groups have a symbiotic relationship with their funding partners. Not only do they receive money from the large foundations, but they even help the foundations craft their strategic programs and mission areas. In some cases, present and/or former leaders from the public interest groups serve as staff or board members of the grant-making foundations.

The liberal public interest groups are also endlessly inventive. Some public interest organizations help the large foundations maximize and coordinate projects by creating innovative conduits both on the funding end in the use of resources and on the execution side of the equation.

A perfect example of this is the Tides Center, which provides financial and other services and resource coordination to public interest groups—particularly small and newly organized local or issue-specific groups—and offers the large grant-making institutions a way to maximize the impact of their philanthropy through this strategic clearinghouse approach. If, for example, two or three groups approach the Tides Center about an environmental justice project in the San Francisco Bay Area, the center can help them coordinate their projects and avoid a duplication of effort, minimize their overhead, and improve their chances with large donors. It can also help the grant-making organizations advance their strategic goals more effectively by helping them vet potential grant recipients and serving as a conduit between the grantors and the recipients.

Three of the largest and most activist organizations—the American Civil Liberties Union, People for the American Way, and the Natural Resources Defense Council—epitomize the position enjoyed by liberal public interest law in the opening years of the 21st century. These three groups also indicate how extreme the Left has become, as well as how irrational many of the initiatives undertaken by the liberal public interest movement have become, and reinforce the need for conservative public interest legal groups to counter the rising tide of liberal legal advocacy.

The American Civil Liberties Union

The ACLU is, in many ways, the pioneer of liberal public interest law. Founded in 1920 by a group that included Clarence Darrow, Helen Keller, and a host of liberal activists, union organizers, and communists and socialists, the ACLU has played a role in many of the highest profile civil rights cases in the past century. Some, like *Brown v. Board of Education*, were pivotal in advancing social and cultural understanding regarding race in America, but the ACLU also has a history of taking on extremist causes and clients that appear to have little to do with the preservation of individual rights.

These include the Sacco and Vanzetti case in the 1920s; the defense of Nazis' right to assemble in Skokie, Illinois; and the defense of the pedophilia advocacy group NAMBLA (North American Man–Boy Love Association) in Boston in 2000. In another recent case, the ACLU defended an effort by an atheist to have the Boy Scouts of America banned from public schools in Portland, Oregon, purportedly because the Scouts can deny membership to young people who do not profess a relationship with God.

In other instances, the group has abandoned the pretense of protecting civil liberties entirely and simply promoted its political agenda. After the 2000 presidential election, the ACLU was one of the leading sponsors of a project called Transition Watch, an Internet initiative designed to oppose the early phases of the Bush administration. The ACLU also filed suit in California in 2003 to block the recall of then-Governor Gray Davis.

According to its Web site, the ACLU has nearly 400,000 dues-paying members nationwide. The group also receives funds from many of the nation's top liberal grant-makers, such as Ford, Packard, and Kellogg.

People for the American Way

People for the American Way began in 1980 as an idea for a movie about evangelists like Jerry Falwell and Pat Robertson, but television producer Norman Lear (*All in the Family*, *Maude*, *The Jeffersons*) instead decided to take his indictment of conservative theologians a step farther and start an activist organization that would take on conservatives in both the mass media and public policy arenas. People for the American Way launched several national and targeted advertising and public education campaigns to defeat Reagan administration judicial appointments and legal initiatives. In 1985, the group formed its legal defense fund to undertake litigation in addition to its public outreach efforts.

People for the American Way has conducted extensive campaigns to defeat the nominations of Robert Bork and Clarence Thomas to the Supreme Court, as well as hundreds of conservative and Republican candidates for elective office around the nation. It also has carried out voter registration drives and partnered with other liberal groups like the NAACP to defeat school voucher initiatives. A program called Right Wing Watch was formed to monitor the activities of conservative groups like the Christian Coalition and others. The organization also interjected itself into the judicial and media battles in Florida in the aftermath of the 2000 election and played an active role in the fight to defeat John Ashcroft's nomination to be attorney general of the United States.

In 2003, People for the American Way had a budget of approximately $12 million, as well as a staff of 100, and received funding from several of the largest grant-making foundations in the country.[24]

THE AMERICAN CIVIL LIBERTIES UNION

For over 70 years, the American Civil Liberties Union has believed that it is wise not to put any limits on freedom of association. It has insisted that the free speech rights of democrats are jeopardized when the free speech rights of terrorists are curbed. This radical libertarian position is simply not possible in the post–September 11 reality of the United States.

The ACLU has been described as "anti-victim" because it presses so hard for the rights of the accused and the convicted without expressing similar concern for the rights of victims. In 1983, for example, it sought to sue prison officials in New York State on behalf of inmates who rioted and were "brutalized" for their violence. An ACLU official explained that "the citizens' right to be free from criminal activity ... is not, in the legal sense, a 'right' at all (and thus is nowhere mentioned in the Bill of Rights) but is, rather, an essential social good, like fire prevention."

The ACLU has become a major player in the Supreme Court nomination process, often employing emotional and even apocalyptic language in opposition to a proposed candidate. It warned its members in 1987 that confirmation of Robert Bork "would threaten our system of government."

The ACLU not only objects to laws that proscribe adultery, cohabitation, and gay and lesbian marriages, but also has sought to legalize polygamy. This is a reversal, says William Donohue, of a long-standing ACLU position that a community's interest in maintaining monogamous relationships may legitimately override individual preferences for polygamy. Its goal is "a constitutional juggernaut" that can topple a host of laws regarding all of the above in numerous states.[1]

To the ACLU, the First Amendment speaks more directly to freedom *from* religion than it does to freedom *of* religion. Former Executive Director Ira Glasser contended that a voucher system in education would have been resisted by the Founders. The ACLU has opposed as unconstitutional the right of Congress to maintain its chaplains; the inscription "In God We Trust" on coins and postage; formal diplomatic relations with the Vatican; kosher inspectors on the payroll of Miami Beach; legislation that criminalizes damage to religious buildings and artifacts; and the right of a judge to order a person found guilty of drunk driving to attend meetings of Alcoholics Anonymous.

The ACLU has maintained since the 1930s that property rights have "nothing to do with the maintenance of democratic processes." This position directly contradicts the fact that property rights are clearly delineated in the Fifth Amendment of the Bill of Rights—the ACLU's "only client."

It is worth noting, writes Donohue, that the ACLU vigorously defends substantive due process regarding First Amendment rights but is markedly hostile to such process when it comes to Fifth Amendment rights.

While professing a profound respect for the Constitution, and especially the Bill of Rights, the ACLU errs badly when it asserts that the Founders believed that individual liberty was the highest common good. Political scientist Clinton Rossiter more accurately captured the central message of Jefferson, Madison, Adams, Washington, *et al.*: "No happiness without liberty, no liberty without self-government, no self-government without constitutionalism, no constitutionalism without morality—and none of these great goods without stability and order."[2]

Lee Edwards

---

[1] William A. Donohue, *Twilight of Liberty: The Legacy of the ACLU* (New Brunswick, N.J.: Transaction Publishers, 1994), p. 45.

[2] *Ibid.*, p. 320.

Natural Resources Defense Council

The Natural Resources Defense Council was founded in 1970 and declares that its goals are:

> to safeguard the Earth: its people, its plants and animals and the natural systems on which all life depends. We work to restore the integrity of the elements that sustain life—air, land and water—and to defend endangered natural places. We seek to establish sustainability and good stewardship of the Earth as central ethical imperatives of human society.[25]

The group focuses on clean air and water, global warming, urban pollution issues (such as brown fields), wildlife preservation, and other environmental issues. It has also taken on the proliferation of nuclear weapons and nuclear waste. The NRDC advances its objectives through lobbying, public education, and mass media campaigns.

In 1989, however, it became the poster child for junk science and gutter tactics with its infamous campaign claiming that the chemical Alar, once used in the treatment of apples, caused cancer in children. The media blitz (including a roll-out with a major story on *60 Minutes*) cost American apple growers, food distributors, and supermarket chains more than $250,000,000. In the end, it turned out that the NRDC's claims were unfounded: The charges that Alar caused thousands of cases of childhood cancer were false.

In addition to the millions that it receives from the leading grant-making foundations such as Packard, Hewlett, Starr, and MacArthur, the Natural Resources Defense Council has more than 500,000 members around the world and operates an aggressive direct mail program. The organization has also garnered support from numerous liberal luminaries and Hollywood celebrities like director/actor Rob Reiner.

Conclusion

It is indisputable that the liberal public interest law movement, with its immense funding from some of America's most important grant-making foundations, has a significant advantage over its conservative counterparts. It is also clear, from the victories conservatives have won in recent years, that the force of the conservative cause—defending the founding principles of the American republican system of governance and fighting to preserve individual liberty, free speech, free enterprise, and personal expression—possesses philosophical strengths that its opponents still fail to understand.

---

[1] Ford Foundation Web site, at *http://www.fordfound.org*.

[2] *Ibid.*

[3] *Ibid.*

[4] Grantee information derived from Capital Research Center, *CRCSearchlight*, at *http://www.capitalresearch.org/search/gmdisplay.asp?Org=131684331*.

[5] Lucille Packard died in 1987.

[6] David and Lucille Packard Foundation, Consolidated Financial Statements for the Year Ended December 31, 2002 and Independent Auditor's Report, at *http://www.packard.org*.

[7] David and Lucille Packard Foundation Web site, at *http://www.packard.org*.

[8] *Ibid.*

[9] Grantee information derived from Capital Research Center, *CRCSearchlight*, at *http://www.capitalresearch.org/search/gmdisplay.asp?Org=942278431*.

[10] William and Flora Hewlett Foundation Web site, at *http://www.hewlett.org*.

[11] *Ibid.*

[12] *Ibid.*

[13] *Ibid.*

[14] Capital Research Center Web site, at *http://www.capitalresearch.org/search/gmdisplay.asp?Org=941655673*.

[15] W. K. Kellogg Foundation Web site, at *http://www.wkkf.org*.

[16] *Ibid.*

[17] *Chronicle of Philanthropy* Web site, at *http://www.philanthropy.com/premium/stats/foundation/2003/2003_results.php?searchType=2*.

[18] *Ibid.*

[19] Capital Research Center, *CRCSearchlight*, at *http://www.capitalresearch.org/ search/gmdisplay.asp?Org=381359264.*

[20] Starr Foundation, IRS Form 990, 2001, at *http://fdncenter.org/grantmaker/starr.*

[21] Capital Research Center, *CRCSearchlight*, at *http://www.capitalresearch.org/ search/gmdisplay?Org=136151545.*

[22] John D. and Catherine T. MacArthur Foundation Web site, at *http://www. macfdn.org.*

[23] Capital Research Center, *CRCSearchlight*, at *http://www.capitalresearch.org/ search/gmdisplay.asp?Org=237093598.*

[24] Bob Davis and Robert S. Greenberger, "Two Old Foes Plot Tactics in Battle Over Judgeships," *The Wall Street Journal*, March 2, 2004.

[25] Natural Resources Defense Council, "About Us: Mission Statement," at *www.nrdc.org.*

CHAPTER 10

The Revival of Federalism

John C. Eastman[1]

In late 1940, still reeling from the effects of the Great Depression on his small dairy farm in Montgomery County, Ohio, Roscoe Filburn sowed on his own land and later harvested 23 acres of winter wheat, some of which he used to feed his chickens and cows, some of which he used for making flour for home consumption, and some of which he saved as seed for the following season. For this, he was fined by the federal government because he had grown more wheat on his farm than federal law allowed.

Specifically, regulations issued by Agriculture Secretary Claude Wickard pursuant to the Agricultural Adjustment Act of 1938 limited Filburn to 11.1 acres of wheat at a normal yield of 20.1 bushels of wheat per acre. Filburn harvested 462 bushels of wheat from the 23 acres, or 239 bushels more than his allotment—an illegal "farm marketing excess" under the act and its implementing regulations.

Filburn may have thought the law could not possibly apply to him. After all, the putative source of the federal government's authority was the power of Congress "to regulate commerce among the states." Filburn was not selling the wheat at issue, so he was not engaged in commerce of any kind, much less interstate commerce. His harvest could hardly be deemed a "marketing excess" when none of it was sent to market.

Nevertheless, the Supreme Court in 1942 unanimously upheld the federal law and the fine imposed on Filburn. Had Filburn not chosen to use his own wheat, he would have purchased wheat from others; his decision *not* to enter the wheat market, therefore, when aggregated with the similar decisions of countless other farmers throughout the country trying, literally, to put bread on their own families' tables, had a substantial enough effect on the interstate market in wheat to render the law constitutional.

Following on a handful of other New Deal-era decisions by the Supreme Court that expansively interpreted the Interstate Commerce Clause[2] and repudiated a slew of decisions that had been rendered by the Court over the previous 50 years,[3] *Wickard v. Filburn*[4] stood for the proposition that Congress had virtually unlimited power to regulate the nation's economic as well as non-economic activity. Congress could regulate the price of milk produced and sold within a single state because of the effect it would have on commerce.[5] It could regulate the wages earned and hours worked by employees of manufacturing facilities in a single state if any of the goods were later shipped in (or even affected) interstate commerce.[6] And it could regulate, under its "commerce among the states" power, any wholly intrastate activity that was downstream from a transaction that had, at one time, involved interstate commerce.[7]

Together, these New Deal cases sanctioned the view that, in addition to interstate commerce itself, Congress could regulate any activity that might one day result in commerce, as well as any activity that utilized goods that had previously moved in commerce. In other words, Congress could regulate virtually anything it chose to regulate, and it took the unlimited power to heart. Even the supposedly conservative President Richard Nixon joined it in even more expansive exertions of federal power such as the Clean Water Act of 1972 and the Endangered Species Act of 1973.

Regulating Puddles

The regulatory agencies, too, became drunk on the Commerce Clause aphrodisiac. The U.S. Army Corps of Engineers, for example, acting pursuant to a statute designed to protect the flow of commerce through the navigable waterways of the United States, contended that it had the power to regulate a proposed local landfill because migratory birds sometimes stopped to bathe in the puddles that developed after a rain in the gravel pit that was to be the site of the landfill. In another case, the Corps successfully prosecuted the owner of a truck repair shop for removing some old tires from and adding fill dirt to his land so that he could expand his garage. The land became soggy during Pennsylvania's rainy season and therefore was a "wetland," which, according to the Corps, qualified as a "navigable water" of the United States, necessitating a Clean Water Act permit before fill dirt—a "pollutant" under the Act—could be added.[8]

The Environmental Protection Agency, acting pursuant to the same Clean Water Act, imposed massive fines on a farmer for plowing his own fields in central California, based on the view that the farmer's plowing prevented run-off of water that, when aggregated with the run-off from other un-plowed farms, would form a streamlet, and then a stream, and ultimately make its way—God willing and the sun don't shine (too warmly, that is)—into a navigable waterway.[9]

After *Wickard*, there was virtually no judicial check on the exercise of the federal government's Commerce Clause power. By 1978, Harvard Law Professor Laurence Tribe, one of the nation's leading constitutional law scholars, would write that "The Supreme Court has ... largely abandoned any effort to articulate and enforce *internal* limits on congressional power—limits inherent in the grants of power themselves."[10] Professor Gerald Gunther would write in the tenth edition of his constitutional law textbook shortly thereafter that, "After nearly 200 years of government under the Constitution, there are very few judicially enforced checks on the congressional commerce power." Indeed, *Wickard*'s view of the Commerce Clause was so pervasive that generations of law school students were not even taught that there might be another constitutional interpretation to consider.

According to the received wisdom, the correct view had been articulated in the 1824 case of *Gibbons v. Ogden*, in which Chief Justice John Marshall had written that the Commerce Clause gave the federal government power to regulate not just interstate commerce, but all "commerce which concerns more states than one," including wholly intrastate commerce that had an effect in other states (which meant, in the modern world, just about everything). The 50-year period leading up to *Wickard* in which the Court strictly interpreted the clause to reach only "commerce" (in contrast to agriculture or manufacturing, on the one hand, or retail sales, on the other) that was truly "interstate" (in contrast to wholly *intra*state), if taught at all, was taught as a naïve aberration from the Founders' vision (as articulated by Marshall) of a laissez-faire-motivated Court that was finally buried once and for all with *Wickard*. "The view of the commerce clause developed by the Court" between 1887 and 1937, wrote Tribe matter-of-factly, "contrasted sharply with the approach of Marshall in *Gibbons v. Ogden*."[11]

The Scholarly Effort

All of this demonstrates just how enormous is the task of restoring the original understanding of the Commerce Clause and reviving any sense of limits on the awesome power of the federal government. This was one of the key tasks undertaken at the outset by the pro-freedom public interest law movement, but litigation strategies alone would not accomplish the mission. The Founders' original vision was all but lost to the academic world and, hence, to the jurisprudential world that drew heavily from it. A scholarly recovery effort would also have to be undertaken, laying the groundwork for the litigation efforts.

It is thus no accident that the same year the Pacific Legal Foundation opened its doors, in 1973, The Heritage Foundation was formed as a research and educational think tank "whose mission is to formulate and promote conservative public policies based on the principles of free enterprise, limited government, individual freedom, traditional American values, and a strong national defense." Within five years, the Claremont Institute for the Study of Statesmanship and Political Philosophy was formed with the explicit mission "to restore the principles of the American founding to their rightful, preeminent authority in our national life." The Reason Foundation and the Cato Institute, with their more libertarian bent, were formed to support the rule of law, private property, and limited government.

In 1982, the Federalist Society was formed, designed to revive or at least reopen the debate about the Founders' vision in the very belly of the beast, the nation's law schools. Today, the society's student division numbers more than 5,000 law students at roughly 145 of the nation's 168 ABA-accredited law schools; its lawyers division counts more than 20,000 legal professionals in its ranks; and its faculty division, formed in 1999, is testament to the growing influence on law school campuses of those who seek to restore the principles of the American founding to the law school corpus.

The archeology of the Founders' views undertaken by these scholarly think tanks was a critical component of the pro-freedom public interest law movement's assault on the New Deal's citadel of unlimited federal power. Below, with particular focus on the Commerce Clause itself, is what that archeology uncovered, which is now serving as the basis for further litigation efforts.

The Founders' Vision Unearthed

When the Framers of our Constitution met in Philadelphia in 1787, it was widely acknowledged that a stronger national government than existed under the Articles of Confederation was necessary if the new government of the United States was going to survive. The Continental Congress could not honor its commitments under the

Treaty of Paris; it could not meet its financial obligations; and it could not insure that its citizens, especially those living on the western frontier, were secure in their lives and property.

Perhaps of greatest concern, though, was the inability of the central government to counteract the crippling trade barriers that were being enacted by the several states against each other, for the Framers rightly perceived that the disputes over commerce threatened the national unity that was critically important to the survival of the new nation.[12] Indeed, the first convention called to address problems with the Articles of Confederation, held at Annapolis in 1786, was specifically devoted to concerns about interstate commerce and navigation. There was, thus, general agreement about the need to give to the national government more power over interstate commerce.

But the Framers were equally cognizant of the fact that the deficiencies of the Articles of Confederation existed by design, due to a genuine and almost universal fear of a strong, centralized government.[13] Our forebears had not successfully prosecuted the war against the king's tyranny merely to erect another form of tyranny in its place.

The central problem faced by the convention delegates, therefore, was to create a government strong enough to meet the threats to the safety and happiness of the people, yet not so strong as to itself become a threat to the people's liberty.[14] The Framers drew on the best political theorists of human history to craft a government that was most conducive to that end. The idea of separation of powers, for example, evident in the very structure of the Constitution, was drawn from Montesquieu out of recognition that the "accumulation of all powers, legislative, executive, and judiciary, in the same hands ... may justly be pronounced the very definition of tyranny."[15]

But the Framers added their own contribution to the science of politics as well. In what can only be described as a radical break with past practice, the Founders rejected the idea that the government was sovereign and indivisible. Instead, they contended that the people themselves were the ultimate sovereign[16] and could delegate all or part of their sovereign powers to a single government or to multiple governments, as, in their view, was "most likely to effect their Safety and Happiness."[17] As a result, it became and remains one of the most fundamental tenets of our constitutional system of government that the sovereign people delegated to the national government only certain, enumerated powers, leaving the residuum of power to be exercised by the state governments or by the people themselves.[18]

This division of sovereign powers between the two great levels of government was not simply a constitutional add-on by way of the Tenth Amendment.[19] Rather, it is inherent in the doctrine of enumerated powers embodied in the main body of the Constitution itself. Article I of the Constitution provides, for example, that "All legislative Powers *herein granted* shall be vested in a Congress of the United States."[20] And the specific enumeration of powers, found principally in Article I, section 8, was likewise limited.

Commerce and the Founders

Perhaps foremost among the powers granted to the national government was the power to regulate commerce among the states; but for the Founders, "commerce" was trade, or commercial intercourse between nations and states, not business activity generally.[21] Indeed, in *Gibbons v. Ogden*, the first major case arising under the clause to reach the Supreme Court, it was contested whether the Commerce Clause even extended so far as to include "navigation." Chief Justice Marshall, for the Court, held that it did, but even under his definition, "commerce" was limited to "intercourse between nations, and parts of nations, in all its branches."[22]

This is a far cry from the expansive reading of Marshall's opinion in *Gibbons* that prevailed after *Wickard* and the other New Deal-era Commerce Clause cases. Rather, the *Gibbons* Court specifically rejected the notion "that [commerce among the states] comprehend[s] that commerce, which is completely internal, which is carried on between man and man in a State, or between different parts of the same State, and which does not extend to or affect other States."[23]

In other words, for Chief Justice Marshall and his colleagues, the Commerce Clause did not even extend to trade carried on between different parts of a state. The notion that the power to regulate commerce among the states included the power to regulate all other kinds of business activity, therefore, was completely foreign to them.

This understanding—the original understanding—of the Commerce Clause continued for nearly a century and a half. Manufacturing was not included in the definition of commerce, held the Court in *United States v. E. C. Knight Co.*,[24] because "Commerce succeeds to manufacture, and is not a part of it." "The fact that an article is manufactured for export to another State does not of itself make it an article of interstate commerce...."[25] Neither were retail sales included in the definition of "commerce."[26]

For the Founders and for the courts that decided these cases, regulation of such activities as retail sales, manufacturing, and agriculture was part of the police powers reserved to the states, not part of the power over commerce delegated to Congress.[27] Moreover, as the Court noted in *E. C. Knight*, it was essential to the preservation of the states—and therefore to liberty—that the line between the two powers be retained:

> It is vital that the independence of the commercial power and of the police power, and the delimitation between them, however sometimes perplexing, should always be recognized and observed, for, while the one furnishes the strongest bond of union, the other is essential to the preservation of the autonomy of the States as required by our dual form of government....[28]

The Litigation Front

The original view of the Commerce Clause described above, recovered by the think tanks and ultimately in the legal literature,[29] would have to be recovered as a jurisprudential matter as well if there was to be any chance at restoring a federal government of only limited, enumerated powers.

Much more than constitutional purity was at stake. The Founders believed that centralized government would tend to become tyrannical, but they also thought it would become unaccountable and inefficient. As with the notoriously erroneous five-year plans of Stalin's Soviet Union, command-and-control bureaucracies are simply not good either at balancing costs and benefits or at getting right the incentives necessary for good policymaking. Indeed, in many instances, they may be legally incapable of even considering the economic costs of their regulatory policies.

Two news items of 2003 highlight the nature of the problem. Because of the absolutist nature of the Endangered Species Act, the U.S. Fish and Wildlife Service has demanded that extraordinary efforts be made to protect the silvery minnow in Colorado, including the refusal to release water to downstream users from the reservoirs that serve as the minnow's habitat. The Service's demands exacerbated the drought conditions in northern New Mexico, leaving an insufficient supply of water for the region's pinyon trees. Without enough water, the trees were unable to produce sap, their primary defense against insects. The result was a bark beetle infestation that, by latest estimates, will destroy between 80 percent and 85 percent of the region's pinyon trees and has already destroyed 96 percent of the trees in some higher elevation areas.[30]

Even more troubling were the October 2003 California wildfires. The Endangered Species Act was again the culprit. Required by law to protect species habitat to the exclusion of all else, the

U.S. Fish and Wildlife Service prevented California officials from implementing prudent forestry management tools because of a putative threat to southwestern arroyo toad habitat, leaving southern California's forests a tinderbox of excessive growth and dead brush. The tragic irony: In addition to the loss of human life and property, much of the sacrosanct species habitat was itself destroyed by the fires.[31]

Leading the litigation charge, as in other areas, was Ronald Zumbrun and the Pacific Legal Foundation. Founded in 1973, the foundation began its Commerce Clause litigation efforts as early as 1975 when, in the case of *Kleppe v. New Mexico*,[32] Zumbrun and another foundation attorney, John Findley, filed an *amicus curiae* brief contending that the Wild Free-roaming Horses and Burrows Act of 1971[33] exceeded Congress's Commerce Clause power. The federal government's unconstitutional regulation protected wild horses and jackasses not just on federal lands, but on private lands as well, without any connection to interstate commerce.

The Pacific Legal Foundation's brief provided a good description of the consequences: "As a result of the legislation, the animals are completely unrestrained and are allowed to roam at will onto private property resulting in the destruction of crops, the depletion of food supplies provided for livestock, and the injury and harassment of livestock." The federal law was ultimately upheld as a valid exercise of the federal government's power under the Lands Clause—the jackasses won the first round—but the foundation had begun the Commerce Clause recovery effort.[34]

It took a hearty band of litigators at Pacific Legal Foundation and elsewhere, though, to maintain this effort as the original Commerce Clause views espoused by the foundation and its pro-liberty allies met with one defeat after another, much as Thurgood Marshall's early efforts to recover the promise of equality contained in the Declaration of Independence but repudiated in the ignominious decision of *Plessy v. Ferguson* were repeatedly rebuffed by the courts.

In *Hodel v. Indiana*,[35] for example, the Supreme Court upheld the prime farmland provisions of the Surface Mining Control and Reclamation Act of 1977,[36] which required that surface-mined prime farmland be returned to prime farmland condition once mining operations were completed—necessitating, among other things, that the land be returned to its original contours after the completing of mining operations, a process that rendered most surface mining projects economically unfeasible. John Cannon of the Mid-Atlantic Legal Foundation, founded in 1975, filed an *amicus* brief contending that the prime farmland provisions of the 1977 act exceeded Congress's authority under the Commerce Clause.[37]

Cannon contended that the provisions went even further than the wheat marketing orders of the Agricultural Adjustment Act, upheld in *Wickard v. Filburn*, because they regulated *only* local activity without any pretense of connection to a regulation of interstate commerce itself. Although the federal district court had agreed that the act's prime farmland provisions exceeded Congress's Commerce Clause power, the Supreme Court unanimously rejected the claim, reiterating its broad view of the power conferred by the Commerce Clause:

> A court may invalidate legislation enacted under the Commerce Clause only if it is clear that there is no rational basis for a congressional finding that the regulated activity affects interstate commerce, or that there is no reasonable connection between the regulatory means selected and the asserted ends.[38]

Amicus curiae briefs raising a combination of Commerce Clause and Tenth Amendment challenges to the Public Utility Regulatory Policy Act of 1978 (PURPA)[39] were filed in the 1982 case of *F.E.R.C. v. Mississippi*[40] by the Southeastern Legal Foundation, founded in 1976, and the Mountain States Legal Foundation, founded in 1977. Southeastern's legal crew of Ben Blackburn, Wayne Elliott, Allen Hirons, and Stephen Parker contended that "PURPA does not regulate directly energy or commerce in energy. Instead, PURPA regulates sovereign state governmental activities which, by their very nature, are not subject to the Commerce Power."

Mountain States Legal Foundation's legal team of Roger Marzulla, Gale Norton (later to become Secretary of the Interior), and Alison Noven pointed out that the act "does not regulate commerce itself but attempts to regulate the manner in which states exercise their legislative, judicial and executive power to regulate public utilities." Indeed, the foundation noted, "the procedural rules imposed by PURPA are so specific that they even tell the state commission what it may charge for transcripts."

Although the anti-commandeering position advanced in these briefs would subsequently prevail a decade later in *New York v. United States*, it was rejected by the Court in *F.E.R.C.*, by a margin of 6 to 3, as "somewhat novel." Justice O'Connor (who would later author the majority opinion in *New York v. United States*), joined by Chief Justice Burger and Justice Rehnquist, dissented on the Court's Tenth Amendment analysis but "agreed with the Court that the Court's Commerce Clause supported" PURPA.

The Thomas "Swamp"

Pacific Legal Foundation's Ron Zumbrun, Sam Kazman, and Kevin Heron also filed an *amicus* brief in *United States v. Riverside Bayview Homes, Inc.*,[41] contending that the extension of the federal Clean Water Act's definition of "navigable waters" to cover backyard swamps exceeded the Commerce Clause power. The Pacific Legal Foundation's description of the case is particularly enlightening:

> In 1981, Mr. Thomas extended his backyard an additional 8 feet to his property line by filling in a "swamp" area with 50 cubic yards of dirt. He then planted grass seed and started a vegetable garden on the filled-in land. The [U.S. Army Corps of Engineers] asserted Section 404 jurisdiction over the property and ordered Mr. Thomas either to remove the dirt or apply for an "after-the-fact" Section 404 permit.

Thomas decided to submit a permit application, which contained as one of its 55 questions what the effect of the project would be on navigation. The "swamp" Thomas filled had previously been a breeding ground for rodents and mosquitoes and was not connected to any other body of water, navigable or otherwise. Yet a unanimous Supreme Court nevertheless found the Corps' assertion of jurisdiction over Thomas's backyard swamp to be a valid exercise of Congress' power to regulate commerce among the states.

Ron Zumbrun, of the Pacific Legal Foundation, this time joined by fellow foundation attorneys Edward Connor, Jr., and John Groen, also participated in *Preseault v. Interstate Commerce Commission*,[42] which involved the federal "Rails to Trails" program that essentially obliterated the reversionary interests of private property owners in abandoned railroad easements. The Court unanimously upheld the federal program against a Commerce Clause challenge by petitioners in the case, but so thoroughly had the Commerce Clause claims been repudiated by the Court in prior cases that the foundation rested its argument on the Takings Clause rather than the Commerce Clause.

Similarly, in *Gregory v. Ashcroft*,[43] the Washington Legal Foundation's Daniel Popeo and John Scully declined even to advance a Commerce Clause challenge to the federal Age Discrimination in Employment Act, which was relied upon by Missouri State Court judges to challenge Missouri's mandatory retirement age. Although the Supreme Court held that the act could not be applied to state court judges, it did so on Tenth Amendment grounds without even a hint of Commerce Clause concern, thus leaving Congress free to regulate private-sector retirement ages and a whole host of other employment regulations that had been held unconstitutional prior to the New Deal judicial revolution.

The 20-year effort to restore limits to the Commerce Clause finally bore fruit, however, with the Supreme Court's decision in *United States v. Lopez* and its progeny, *United States v. Morrison*, and *Solid Waste Agency of Northern Cook County v. U.S. Army Corps of Engineers.* By then, the Pacific Legal Foundation had a number of allies, including the Texas Justice Foundation, headed by Allan Parker, which, like Pacific Legal, filed an *amicus curiae* brief in *Lopez*; the Center for Individual Rights, founded in 1989, which pursued the Commerce Clause challenge in *Morrison* all the way to argument in the Supreme Court; the Washington Legal Foundation; the Cato Institute; the Institute for Justice; Defenders of Property Rights, led by Roger Marzulla and Nancy Marzulla; and the newest entry, the Center for Constitutional Jurisprudence, the public interest wing of the Claremont Institute founded in 1999. All filed *amicus curiae* briefs in one or more of these landmark cases, articulating the Founders' view of the Commerce Clause and urging the Court to restore the original limits to the Commerce Clause power.

In *Lopez* itself, Ron Zumbrun, Anthony "Tom" Caso, and John Schmidt, Jr., contended in the *amicus* brief filed by the Pacific Legal Foundation, and Professor Clayton Trotter contended in the *amicus* brief filed by the Texas Justice Foundation, that the federal Gun Free School Zone Act, which prohibited gun possession near a school, exceeded Congress's power under the Commerce Clause. More than 20 years after the Pacific Legal Foundation opened its doors and started making such arguments, the Supreme Court finally struck down a federal law on Commerce Clause grounds.

The battle was hardly won, however. Scores of federal statutes and hundreds, perhaps thousands, of federal regulations were invalid under any faithful application of the *Lopez* holding, yet the lower courts continued uniformly to reject Commerce Clause challenges to federal regulatory power in hundreds of cases decided in the immediate aftermath of *Lopez*, resting on the flimsiest of hooks.

For five years, the Supreme Court let the decisions stand, denying *certiorari* in almost every case raising the issue, many of them pursued by the pro-freedom public interest law movement.

Indeed, the Supreme Court itself rejected a strong Commerce Clause challenge pressed by the Washington Legal Foundation's Daniel Popeo and Shawn Gunnerson and the Pacific Legal Foundation's Anne Hayes and Deborah La Freta in *Reno v. Condon*,[44] in which the Court upheld the Driver's Privacy Protection Act.

Finally, in a case defended by Michael Rosman and Hans Bader of the Center for Individual Rights, Judge J. Michael Luttig, writing for an *en banc* majority of the Court of Appeals for the Fourth Circuit, held that the Violence Against Women Act (VAWA) exceeded Congress's Commerce Clause power, all but forcing the Supreme Court to grapple with the implications of its *Lopez* decision. Dozens of briefs were filed in the case, representing hundreds of organizations, most of which urged the Court to reverse the Fourth Circuit (even to overturn *Lopez*) and uphold the Violence Against Women Act.

The Association of Trial Lawyers of America; the Bar Association of the City of New York; Senator Joseph Biden (D–DE); a coalition of self-proclaimed international law scholars and human rights experts; the American Association of University Women; the American Federation of State, County and Municipal Employees, AFL–CIO; a coalition of 100 law professors led by Yale Law School's Bruce Ackerman; and 36 states and the Commonwealth of Puerto Rico were among the hundreds of individuals and organizations that filed briefs in the case in support of the Violence Against Women Act (and of the United States government's own defense of the act).

Arrayed against them was the state of Alabama (represented by its Attorney General William Pryor, later nominated to the Eleventh Circuit Court of Appeals, and Jeff Sutton, later confirmed to the Sixth Circuit Court of Appeals); a couple of policy groups; and a small handful of public interest law firms: Rosman and Bader for the Center for Individual Rights, representing the respondent in the case; former Attorney General Edwin Meese III and John Eastman for the Claremont Institute Center for Constitutional

Jurisprudence; William "Chip" Mellor and Clint Bolick of the Institute for Justice and Roger Pilon, Timothy Lynch, and Robert Levy of the Cato Institute, together with University of Chicago Professor Richard Epstein; and Anne Hayes and Reed Hopper for the Pacific Legal Foundation.

THE FEDERALIST SOCIETY

Founded in 1982, the Federalist Society is not a litigating organization, but it has contributed significantly to the freedom-based public interest law movement. The contributions fall into two categories: those activities that have contributed directly to the legal success of the movement and those that have helped create a legal culture more receptive to the ideas of the movement.

First, the more than 200 Federalist Society chapters (60 for lawyers, 145 at law schools) host speeches and debates involving leaders of the freedom-based public interest law movement and their current cases. These meetings have for many years provided an opportunity for lawyers to test their arguments and for cases to receive publicity.

Second, Federalist Society lawyers who wish to do pro bono work often serve as local counsel or otherwise link up with the freedom-based law firms to work on cases of interest to them. In a similar way, some academics connected with the Federalist Society have become involved with the freedom-based public interest law firms through contacts that originated through Federalist events, chapters, or practice groups.

Third, the Federalist Society has served as an excellent recruiting ground for the freedom-based public interest law movement. The majority of those hired by movement firms over the past two decades have been involved in Federalist Society chapters. Interest may be sparked by a speech hosted by the student's law school chapter, or by a Federalist Student Leadership conference or some other event. In either case, the Federalist Society makes possible the initial connection that is then developed by the public interest law firm.

Fourth, the Federalist Society's Amlaw 100 study provides hard data showing how difficult it is for lawyers interested in freedom-based cases to find such cases. In the future, the Federalist Society will be contributing even more to the movement because it is setting up a Pro Bono Resource Center to facilitate pro bono work through a sophisticated computer system that will match lawyers interested in pro bono work with cases that, while meritorious, firms do not have the resources to handle. The system will also help the firms find local counsel wherever they need it.

In what may well be its greatest contribution to the movement, the Federalist Society has brought freedom-based ideas to every area of the law. This includes the academy, which influences America's future lawyers, judges, and public officials. Members of the freedom-based movement have never had as receptive a climate for their ideas as they would wish. In many areas, however, the climate has improved, and ideas that once were ignored or dismissed now receive a serious hearing.

During the 1980s and early 1990s, the Federalist Society developed 100 chapters in law schools while working with sympathetic professors. Increasingly, the Society's programs and publications have helped to educate leaders on the bench, in the bar, at law schools, and even in the media and public policy worlds. As a result, legal theories based on often neglected constitutional principles have gained more adherents—a trend that has continued and expanded in some areas of the law over the past 15 years. Even in areas where trends have been less favorable, the range of serious ideas includes many that were not part of the legal landscape 20 or 30 years ago.

The Federalist Society's meetings and symposiums are attended by federal and state judges, members of the media, influential law professors, and leading lawyers. In addition, its publications—*Class Action Watch, State Court Docket Watch,* and *Harvard Journal of Law and Public Policy*—are read by members of the judiciary, both federal and state, across the country.

Under Executive Director Eugene Meyer, the Federalist Society not only has helped to identify law students and lawyers who share constitutional principles, but also has developed a community that helps to identify issues calling for litigation. It has encouraged those who share these principles to become involved, whether as freedom-based public interest lawyers or in other capacities. It has provided opportunities for many federal and state judges to hear programs that include the ideas of many freedom-based firms. And it has encouraged many of its members to consider various forms of public service including judicial service.

All of this activity has helped to alter the nation's legal culture and to produce a climate within which it is easier for the freedom-based public interest law firms to carry out their mission with an increased chance of success.

Eugene Meyer

The Commerce Clause Showdown

This was the showdown over the Commerce Clause that had been nearly 30 years in the making. This was the case that would demonstrate whether *Lopez* was merely a historical anomaly, or whether the Court truly intended to enforce the constitutional limits of the Commerce Clause. It was what is known in the legal profession as a "bad facts" case.

Morrison was a Virginia Tech football player accused of raping college co-ed Christy Brzonkala after getting her drunk at a fraternity party. He was initially suspended by the university, but the suspension was subsequently overturned and he was allowed to return to school (and to the football team). The state law remedies available to Brzonkala seemed to many to be wholly inadequate to the emotional trauma she was alleged to have suffered.

What is more, in the wake of *Lopez*, Congress had taken special care to include in the Violence Against Women Act's legislative history lots of testimony about how violence against women affects interstate commerce. The flaw with the Gun Free School Zone act in *Lopez*, it was believed, was that Congress had not articulated the effect on commerce that would have allowed the Court to sustain the act. On this view, *Lopez* would be rendered meaningless, merely requiring Congress to go through some additional legislative hearing hoops before getting back to the "we can regulate whatever we want" *Wickard* view of the Constitution.

The Supreme Court, again by a margin of 5 to 4, rejected these attempts to marginalize *Lopez*. The Violence Against Women Act had nothing to do with commerce and was therefore not a proper exercise of Congress's Commerce Clause power. All of the effects on commerce identified in the legislative history were simply too attenuated, too indirect, to sustain an exertion of power that could essentially supplant the entire criminal law of the 50 states.

If *Lopez* was the Commerce Clause version of *Sweatt v. Painter*,[45] *Morrison* was its *Brown v. Board of Education*.[46] Surely, now the lower courts would get the message that the Court meant what it said in *Lopez*: There were constitutional limits to the Commerce Clause that the courts were required to enforce.

The opportunity would come quickly. Pending in the Fourth Circuit—the Circuit whose holding of the Violence Against Women Act's unconstitutionality had promoted the Supreme Court's decision in *Morrison*—was a case addressing whether the Endangered Species Act could, under the Commerce Clause, validly be extended to a species in which there had not been any known commerce for over a hundred years. Particularly at issue was whether the federal government could criminally prosecute a farmer for shooting a red wolf that was threatening livestock on his private property.

The case, *Gibbs v. Babbitt*,[47] had already been briefed and argued, with active *amicus* involvement from the public interest law movement,[48] but decision was held pending the Supreme Court's decision in *Morrison*. When that decision came down, invalidating the Violence Against Women Act, most observers thought that the Fourth Circuit would follow suit in the red wolf case.

It was not to be. Over a strong dissent from Judge Luttig, Chief Judge Wilkinson held that the red wolf regulations were a valid regulation of interstate commerce because the farmers and ranchers challenging the regulations "take wolves mainly because they are concerned that the animals pose a risk to commercially valuable livestock and crops," and because without red wolves, there would be "no red wolf related tourism, no scientific research, and no commercial trade in pelts." The Supreme Court's decision in *Morrison* was inapposite, held Wilkinson, because it involved a federal intrusion on state criminal law, not environmental law. Apparently, the *Lopez* revolution did not apply in the environmental context.

So the public interest groups sprang into action again, this time to challenge the Army Corps of Engineers' "migratory bird rule," which extended the Clean Water Act's definition of "navigable waters" to include any standing body of water in which migratory birds might take a drink or a bath, whether or not the water was in any way connected to a navigable stream. The Pacific Legal Foundation, Washington Legal Foundation, Center for Individual Rights, Cato Institute and Institute for Justice, Claremont Institute Center for Constitutional Jurisprudence, and Defenders of Property Rights (founded in 1991) all weighed in with Commerce Clause challenges to the Corps' ridiculous assertion of power in *Solid Waste Agency of Northern Cook County v. U.S. Army Corps of Engineers*.[49]

The list of groups arrayed against them puts the case in context. In addition to the core environmental groups that one would expect (the Environmental Defense Fund, Natural Resources Defense Council, National Wildlife Federation, Chesapeake Bay Foundation, World Wildlife Fund, and Defenders of Wildlife), an eclectic collection of groups—the Anti-Defamation League, People for the American Way Foundation, National Gay and Lesbian Task Force, NOW Legal Defense and Education Fund, National Conference for Community and Justice, Human Rights Campaign, National Coalition Against Domestic Violence, National Federation of Filipino American Associations, India Abroad Center for Political Awareness, National Urban League, National Council of Jewish Women, National Women's Law Center, and American Association of University Women—filed an *amicus curiae* brief, urging the Court to uphold the Corps' migratory bird rule. Actually, the groups didn't care one way or another about the migratory bird rule; but they cared mightily about the Commerce Clause, and in particular about the old *Wickard* holding that Congress could regulate any activity that, in the aggregate, had an effect on commerce.

In *Solid Waste Agency of Northern Cook County*, the Court struck down the "migratory bird rule" as a simple matter of statutory construction, but it left no doubt that its Commerce Clause constitutional analysis in *Lopez* was just as applicable in the environmental context as it was in the criminal law context. It also, however, left ambiguous the issue of how its Commerce Clause analysis was to be applied. As a result, the federal government persists in defending, and the lower courts persist in refusing to give any teeth to their review of, federal regulatory policy having nothing to do with interstate commerce.

With the United States now claiming confusion over the meaning of the words "*adjacent* to navigable waters" in the Clean Water Act, the Pacific Legal Foundation, in *United States v. Rapanos*, is defending John Rapanos, who could be sentenced to federal prison for 16 months for modifying wetlands on his Michigan property even though his property is *20 miles away* from any recognized navigable water. The Pacific Legal Foundation is also supporting James and Rebecca Deaton of Maryland, whose 12-acre parcel is eight miles away from any navigable waters. Unfortunately the foundation's petition for *certiorari* was denied by the Supreme Court in both cases. The recalcitrance continues in the Endangered Species Act context as well. In *GDF Realty Investments, Ltd. v. Norton*, the Fifth Circuit upheld, over a Commerce Clause challenge pressed by the Pacific Legal Foundation as part of its new Endangered Species Act Reform Project, the extension of the Endangered Species Act to a group of Texas cave bugs that have no connection to commerce—or, for that matter, to any other species. The Fifth Circuit denied rehearing *en banc*, over six dissenting votes, in February 2004.

Similarly, in a case that brings us back full circle to the California wildfires discussed at the outset of this chapter, the D.C. Circuit rejected a Commerce Clause challenge to the extension of the ESA to the wholly intrastate, non-commercial southwestern arroyo toad. The challenge in this case, *Rancho Viejo, LLC v. Norton*, had been brought by the Claremont Institute Center for Constitutional Jurisprudence. The Supreme Court denied *certiorari* in March 2004.

It remains to be seen whether the Court is ready to fully apply *Lopez*—and the Founders' original view of the Commerce Clause—in the environmental law context. Even if it is, though, we should not expect it to be the final chapter. The proponents of unlimited federal power seem to have an infinite number of epilogues to offer. One thing is certain, however: The pro-freedom public interest law movement will be ready to answer them.

---

[1] The author has been involved in a number of cases discussed in this article, including *United States v. Morrison*, *Solid Waste Agency of Northern Cook County v. U.S. Army Corps of Engineers*, and *Rancho Viejo, LLC v. Norton*.

[2] *N.L.R.B. v. Jones and Laughlin Steel Corporation*, 301 U.S. 1 (1937); *United States v. Darby*, 312 U.S. 100 (1941).

[3] See, e.g., *Hammer v. Dagenhart*, 247 U.S. 251 (1918); *United States v. E. C. Knight Co.*, 156 U.S. 1 (1895).

[4] 317 U.S. 111 (1942).

[5] *United States v. Wrightwood Dairy Co.*, 315 U.S. 110 (1942).

[6] *United States v. Darby*, 312 U.S. 100 (1941).

[7] See, e.g., *United States v. Sullivan*, 332 U.S. 689 (1948) (upholding conviction for "misbranding" of a Columbus, Georgia, retail druggist who had purchased a 1,000-tablet bottle of sulfathiazole from an Atlanta, Georgia, wholesaler and later sold it in a 12-tablet tin without a warning label, where the wholesaler had purchased his product from a Chicago, Illinois, manufacturer).

[8] *United States v. Pozsgai*, 999 F.2d 719 (3rd Cir. 1993), *cert. denied*, 510 U.S. 1110 (1994).

[9] *Borden Ranch Partnership v. U.S. Army Corps of Engineers*, 261 F.3d 810 (9th Cir. 2001), *aff'd by equally divided Court*, 537 U.S. 99 (2002).

[10] Laurence Tribe, *American Constitutional Law* § 5-1, at 224 (1st ed., 1978).

[11] *Id.* at 307. See also Erwin Chemerinsky, *Constitutional Law* 105–06 (2001) ("Beginning in the 1890s, the Supreme Court took a very different approach to the Commerce Clause than that expressed in *Gibbons v. Ogden*"); Geoffrey R. Stone *et al.*, *Constitutional Law* 140 (2nd ed., 1991) (referring to the broad view of *Gibbons* as the "classical view").

[12] See, e.g., Letter from Tench Coxe to the Virginia Commissioners at Annapolis (Sept. 13, 1786), reprinted in 3 *The Founders' Constitution* 473–74 (P. Kurland and R. Lerner eds., 1987) (noting that duties imposed by the states upon each other were "as great in many instances as those imposed on foreign Articles"); *The Federalist* No. 22, at 144–45 (Hamilton) (C. Rossiter and C. Kesler eds., 1999) (referring to "[t]he interfering and unneighborly regulations in some States," which were "serious sources of animosity and discord" between the States); *New York*, 505 U.S., at 158 ("The defect of power in the existing Confederacy to regulate the commerce between its several members [has] been clearly pointed out by experience") (quoting *The Federalist* No. 42, p. 267 (C. Rossiter ed., 1961)).

[13] See, e.g., *Bartkus v. Illinois*, 359 U.S. 121, 137 (1959) ("the men who wrote the Constitution as well as the citizens of the member States of the Confederation were fearful of the power of centralized government and sought to limit its power"); *Garcia v. San Antonio Metropolitan Transportation*

Authority, 469 U.S. 528, 568–69 (1985) (Powell, J., dissenting, joined by Chief Justice Burger and Justices Rehnquist and O'Connor).

[14] See *The Federalist* No. 51, at 322 (Madison).

[15] *The Federalist* No. 47, at 301 (Madison).

[16] See, e.g., James Wilson, Speech at the Pennsylvania Ratifying Convention (Nov. 26, 1787), reprinted in 2 J. Wilson, *The Works of James Wilson* 770 (R. McCloskey ed., 1967).

[17] Declaration of Independence, ¶ 2.

[18] See, e.g., *The Federalist* No. 39, at 256 (Madison) (noting that the jurisdiction of the federal government "extends to certain enumerated objects only, and leaves to the several States a residuary and inviolable sovereignty over all other objects"); *The Federalist* No. 45, at 292–93 (Madison) ("The powers delegated by the proposed Constitution to the federal government are few and defined. Those which are to remain in the State governments are numerous and indefinite"); *McCulloch v. Maryland*, 17 U.S. (4 Wheat.) 316, 421 (1819) (Marshall, C.J.) ("We admit, as all must admit, that the powers of the government are limited and that its limits are not to be transcended"); *Gregory*, 501 U.S. at 457 ("The Constitution created a Federal Government of limited powers").

[19] See U.S. Const. Amend. X ("The powers not delegated to the United States by the Constitution, nor prohibited by it to the States, are reserved to the States respectively, or to the people").

[20] U.S. Const. Art. I, Sec. 1 (emphasis added); see also Art. I, Sec. 8 (enumerating powers so granted); *McCulloch*, 17 U.S. (4 Wheat.), at 405 ("This government is acknowledged by all, to be one of enumerated powers. The principle, that it can exercise only the powers granted to it...is now universally admitted"); *United States v. Lopez*, 514 U.S. 549, 552 (1995) ("We start with first principles. The Constitution creates a Federal Government of enumerated powers").

[21] See, e.g., *Corfield v. Coryell*, 6 F. Cas. 546, 550 (C.C.E.D.Pa. 1823) (Washington, J., on circuit) ("Commerce with foreign nations, and among the several states, can mean nothing more than intercourse with those nations, and among those states, for purposes of trade, be the object of the trade what it may"); *Lopez*, 514 U.S., at 585 (Thomas, J., concurring) ("At the time the

original Constitution was ratified, 'commerce' consisted of selling, buying, and bartering, as well as transporting for these purposes").

[22] 22 U.S. (9 Wheat.) 1, 190 (1824); see also *Corfield,* 6 F. Cas., at 550 ("Commerce...among the several states...must include all the means by which it can be carried on, [including]...passage over land through the states, where such passage becomes necessary to the commercial intercourse between the states").

[23] *Gibbons,* 22 U.S., at 194 (quoted in *Morrison,* 120 S. Ct., at 1753).

[24] 156 U.S. 1, 12 (1895).

[25] *Id.,* at 13; see also *Kidd v. Pearson,* 128 U.S. 1, 20 (1888) (upholding a state ban on the manufacture of liquor, even though much of the liquor so banned was destined for interstate commerce).

[26] See *The License Cases,* 46 U.S. (5 How.) 504 (1847) (upholding state ban on retail sales of liquor, as not subject to Congress's power to regulate interstate commerce); see also *A.L.A. Schechter Poultry Corp. v. United States,* 295 U.S. 495, 542, 547 (1935) (invalidating federal law regulating in-state retail sales of poultry that originated out of state and fixing the hours and wages of the intrastate employees because the activity related only indirectly to commerce).

[27] See, e.g., *E. C. Knight,* 156 U.S., at 12 ("That which belongs to commerce is within the jurisdiction of the United States, but that which does not belong to commerce is within the jurisdiction of the police power of the State") (citing *Gibbons,* 22 U.S. (9 Wheat.), at 210; *Brown v. Maryland,* 25 U.S. (12 Wheat.) 419, 448 (1827); *The License Cases,* 46 U.S. (5 How.), at 599; *Mobile Co. v. Kimball,* 102 U.S. 691 (1880); *Bowman v. Railway Co.,* 125 U.S. 465 (1888); *Leisy v. Hardin,* 135 U.S. 100 (1890); *In re Rahrer,* 140 U.S. 545, 555 (1891)).

[28] 156 U.S., at 13; see also *Carter Coal,* 298 U.S., at 301 (quoting *E. C. Knight*); *Garcia,* 469 U.S., at 572 (Powell, J., dissenting, joined by Chief Justice Burger and Justices Rehnquist and O'Connor) ("federal overreaching under the Commerce Clause undermines the constitutionally mandated balance of power between the States and the Federal Government, a balance designed to protect our fundamental liberties").

[29] See, e.g., R. Berger, *Federalism: The Founders' Design* 148–51 (1987); R. Bork, *The Tempting of America: The Political Seduction of the Law* 56–57

(1990) (explaining that *Wickard* "abandoned" aspects of the Constitution that defined and limited national power); R. Epstein, *Forbidden Grounds: The Case Against Employment Discrimination Laws* 139 (1992) (contending that *Wickard* was a "manifestly erroneous" decision that left "no conceivable stopping point for the federal commerce power"); L. Graglia, *United States v. Lopez: Judicial Review Under the Commerce Clause*, 74 Tex. L. Rev. 719, 745 (1996) (referring to *Wickard* as a "notorious" decision); C. Sunstein, *Congress, Constitutional Moments, and the Cost-Benefit State*, 48 Stan. L. Rev. 247, 253 and n.18 (1996) (describing *Wickard* as a "repudiation" of the original Constitution that gave the national government "something close to general police powers"); B. Ackerman, *Liberating Abstraction*, 59 U. Chi. L. Rev. 317, 322, 324 (1992) (describing *Wickard* as a "wrenching break with the constitutional past," ringing the "death-knell for traditional notions of limited national government"); *cf.* L. Tribe, *American Constitutional Law*, Vol. 1, p. 831 n.29 (3rd ed., 2000) (describing hypothetical "sham" legislation that could result from the combination of the substantial effects test and the aggregation principle); G. Gunther and K. Sullivan, *Constitutional Law* 191 (13th ed., 1997) (suggesting that *Wickard* "in effect abandon[ed] all judicial concern with federalism-related limits on congressional power").

[30] See *Rio Grande Silvery Minnow v. Keys*, 333 F.3d 1109 (10th Cir. 2003); Tom Sharpe, "Colder Weather Has Not Stopped Beetles," *The Santa Fe New Mexican* (Nov. 11, 2003).

[31] See, e.g., Ben Goad and Jennifer Bowles, "Fire Official Faults Agency," *The Riverside Press-Enterprise*, A1 (Dec. 16, 2003).

[32] 426 U.S. 529 (1976).

[33] 85 Stat. 649, 16 U.S.C. §§ 1331–1340 (1970 ed., Supp. IV).

[34] PLF also argued that the federal law intruded upon state sovereignty. Parallel to the Commerce Clause cases discussed here has been a litigation effort by a number of the same pro-freedom public interest groups to recover the "state sovereignty" aspects of federalism. While the courts have frequently misconstrued the doctrine in cases interpreting the Tenth and Eleventh Amendments, Justice Scalia's holding for the Court in *Printz v. United States*, 521 U.S. 898 (1997), properly addressed the issue as a component of the "proper" requirement in the

Article I, section 9 Necessary and Proper Clause. While related, these sovereign immunity cases are beyond the scope of this chapter.

[35] 452 U.S. 314 (1981).

[36] 91 Stat. 445, 30 U.S.C. § 1201 *et seq.* (1976 ed., Supp. III).

[37] In parallel litigation involving related provisions of the 1977 Act, Ronald Zumbrun, Raymond Momboisse, and Eileen White of the Pacific Legal Foundation contended that the Act violated the Tenth Amendment and the Takings Clause of the Fifth Amendment. Those claims, too, were unanimously rejected by the Court, which continued to treat the Commerce Clause as a virtually unlimited grant of power to Congress. See *Hodel v. Virginia Surface Mining and Reclamation Association, Inc.,* 452 U.S. 264 (1981).

[38] *Hodel v. Indiana,* 452 U.S. at 323–24.

[39] 16 U.S.C. § 2601 *et seq.*

[40] 456 U.S. 742 (1982).

[41] 474 U.S. 121 (1985).

[42] 494 U.S. 1 (1990).

[43] 501 U.S. 452 (1991).

[44] 528 U.S. 141 (2000).

[45] 339 U.S. 629 (1950) (ordering desegregation of University of Texas Law School).

[46] 347 U.S. 483 (1954).

[47] 214 F.3d 483 (2000).

[48] Reed Hopper and Anne Hayes for the Pacific Legal Foundation; Daniel Popeo and Paul Kamenar for the Washington Legal Foundation.

[49] 531 U.S. 159 (2001).

Conclusion

Lee Edwards

As this history has shown, American citizens are freer today because of the many-faceted work of the freedom-based public interest law movement. In key area after key area, pro-freedom legal aid groups have fought for the rights of the people against special interests and overweening government, and they have won—for the people.

The movement is a response to the unsettling fact that, as William H. Mellor of the Institute for Justice has put it, at a time when there is more litigation than ever before, increasing numbers of Americans "are shut out of the legal system." They have no recourse for many legitimate grievances because of the costs and the delays of litigation. They are, Mellor says, "increasingly power-less" to control their own destinies, provide for their families, and enjoy the blessings of liberty. It is these Americans that the freedom-based public interest law movement is committed to representing.

As Edwin Meese III says in his foreword, much has been accomplished on their behalf and for a rule of law based on the principles laid down by the Founding Fathers and the original meaning of the Constitution, but much remains to be done.

In the area of *property rights*, pro-freedom legal organizations led by the Pacific Legal Foundation formulated the legal concept of "regulatory takings," which states that government regulations that significantly restrict land use and lower land value constitute a "taking" just as much as does the government's physical occupation of the land. The foundation's concept won before the Supreme Court in *Nollan v. California Coastal Commission* in 1987 and again in *Dolan v. City of Tigard* in 1994. The foundation, along with other members of the pro-freedom public interest law movement, is resolved to continue defending the interests—and the constitutional rights—of private property owners.

In the area of *school choice*, pro-freedom litigators led by Clint Bolick of the Institute for Justice prevailed in the Supreme Court in *Zelman v. Simmons-Harris* in 2002 with their argument that school choice was about education, not religion. The central issue, they argued, was using such things as school vouchers and tuition tax credits to provide educational opportunities for children, particularly in the inner cities, who urgently need them. When the Supreme Court agreed, Bolick said, "a constitutional cloud" was lifted from school choice, and minority and low-income parents celebrated.

In the area of *religious liberty*, the pro-freedom movement, led by the Alliance Defense Fund since 1994, has provided significant assistance in a number of Supreme Court victories, including *Adler v. Duval County School Board* (upholding the right of students to speak about their faith and pray at graduation); *Good News Club v. Milford Central School* (the club's meetings during non-school hours at school facilities did not violate the Establishment Clause); *Mitchell v. Helms* (state funding to religious schools is constitutional); *Agostini v. Felton* (state funding of remedial education teachers for special-needs children in religious schools does not violate the Establishment Clause); and *Rosenberger v. Rector* (the University of Virginia's refusal to give equal funding to a student's religious publication violated his "right of free speech guaranteed by the First Amendment"). The Alliance Defense Fund and other members of the pro-freedom movement will persist in their legal battle against the American Civil Liberties Union and those "who wish to abolish the freedom to publicly acknowledge God." Likewise, other religious liberty advocates have sought to ensure that the federal government does not demand that visitors to and users of federal land bend their knee to the religion of others by maintaining that some federal land is "sacred" to American Indians and must be treated as sacred by non-Indians.

In the field of *economic liberty*, the Institute for Justice and other movement groups are helping small-scale entrepreneurs—like the Rev. Nathaniel Craigmiles of Tennessee—to earn an honest living free from excessive government regulation. Rev. Craigmiles opened a discount funeral casket store, but within a week the state board of funeral directors ordered that he either close his store or risk fines and even a jail sentence. The institute is fighting to vindicate Rev. Craigmiles' right to economic liberty. The institute's litigation has helped deregulate the cosmetology industry in the District of Columbia and California, and has opened up transportation markets in New York, Denver, Cincinnati, and Indianapolis. After the initial entry into the field by Mountain States Legal Foundation, a host of other freedom-based legal organizations have defended economic liberty against so-called environmental laws and regulations as well as judge-made laws. There has been real progress, but there is still a long way to go.

In the field of *equality under the law*, the freedom-based public interest law movement, led by the Center for Individual Rights, is aggressively challenging state-sponsored racial preferences in public college admissions. Although the Supreme Court in 2003 issued a split decision in *Grutter v. Bollinger*, the center and other pro-freedom organizations continue their legal efforts to eliminate illegal racial preferences on and off the campus. The difference that one organization can make was demonstrated in the Supreme Court's 1995 ruling in *Adarand Constructors, Inc. v. Peña*, won by the Mountain States Legal Foundation. *Time* said that *Adarand* threw into doubt most of the government's affirmative action programs.

In the field of *freedom of speech*, one of the most important decisions protecting voluntary association and free speech came in 2000 with *Boy Scouts of America v. Dale*. The *Dale* decision, says Thor L. Halvorssen, is "a new bulwark" for pluralism and the safeguarding of diverse viewpoints. The Supreme Court's ruling was based on a previous legal precedent set in *Hurley v. Irish-American Gay, Lesbian and Bisexual Group of Boston*, which held that veterans—a private group like the Boy Scouts—did not have to allow homosexual activists to participate in their private St. Patrick's Day parade. The Foundation for Individual Rights in Education, headed by Professor Alan Charles Kors of the University of Pennsylvania, and other freedom-based legal groups are vigorously defending free speech at colleges and universities. Their efforts are beginning to help people understand the importance of addressing the illiberal policies of higher education.

In the field of *workers' rights*, the National Right to Work Legal Defense Foundation over the past five decades has provided free legal aid to about 20,000 individual workers and has assisted more than 368,000 employees through class actions to ensure the right of the American worker to join or not join a labor union—or to pay or not pay union dues—as a condition of employment. Since 2000, the Landmark Legal Foundation has taken aim at the powerful National Education Association, charging that the NEA has failed to comply fully with federal tax and campaign laws.

The freedom-based public interest law movement faces formidable opposition in liberal legal aid groups like the ACLU and People for the American Way, which receive millions of dollars annually from such giant foundations as Ford, Kellogg, and

MacArthur. Ironically, Mark R. Levin of the Landmark Legal Foundation points out, these foundations were started by individuals who never intended that their fortunes would be used "to undermine the economic system and social institutions that fostered their entrepreneurial success." Pro-freedom groups counter the liberal activists with fewer resources and less money, making their "David v. Goliath" victories all the more impressive.

In the field of *federalism*, a continuing strength of the freedom-based public interest law movement is its firm commitment to the U.S. Constitution, including the much-misinterpreted Commerce Clause. Although the Supreme Court in *United States v. Lopez* struck down a federal law on Commerce Clause grounds, the federal government persists in defending its regulatory policies in the area of interstate commerce. The proponents of unlimited federal power keep pushing their envelope, but increasingly they are being met and bested by pro-freedom movement forces.

Non-litigating groups such as the Federalist Society, the National Legal Center for the Public Interest, the Cato Institute's Center for Constitutional Studies, and The Heritage Foundation's Center for Legal and Judicial Studies contribute significantly to public interest law by helping to create a legal culture that is more receptive to the ideas of the pro-freedom legal movement. The Federalist Society, for example, brings freedom-based ideas to every area of the law, including the academy, the judiciary, and private practice. There are now more than 200 Federalist Society chapters; the society's *Harvard Journal of Law and Public Policy* is read widely by members of the federal and state judiciary; and the society is setting up a Pro Bono Resource Center to facilitate pro bono work by right-thinking lawyers through a sophisticated computer system.

Through all these activities, the freedom-based public interest law movement strives unceasingly to bring justice to the people— to safeguard their liberties and protect the Constitution, taking as their motto: "Eternal vigilance is the price of liberty."

ACKNOWLEDGMENTS

This history is the idea of a key founder of the freedom-based public interest law movement, Ed Meese, who has continued to make signal contributions to our nation since leaving the office of attorney general some 15 years ago. I was a little nervous when he asked me to edit and contribute to this volume, as my knowledge of the law is limited to that of a layman. But my concerns quickly disappeared when I encountered the expert knowledge and real enthusiasm of the contributors to this book, who clearly understood they were engaged in a unique project—the first-ever history of the pro-freedom legal movement.

I am indebted to Ronald Zumbrun for reading the entire manuscript and for his always wise suggestions, editorial as well as legal. Todd Gaziano, director of the Center for Legal and Judicial Studies at Heritage, was ever available with an answer when I had a question. Eugene Meyer, Ernest Hueter, Roger Clegg, Walter Weber, and Roger Pilon provided valuable insights about their organizations and the movement. I depended for research help on Heritage interns Sara Butler, Clayton Callen, Geoffrey Preston, and Audrey Jones.

I also wish to acknowledge the impressive professionalism of Heritage's publishing team—Jonathan Larsen, Therese Pennefather, Alex Adrianson, and Camille Culbertson—and the sharp eyes of senior copy editor William Poole, proofreader Andrew Blasko, and senior editor Richard Odermatt. And, as ever, I am grateful to Edwin J. Feulner, president of The Heritage Foundation, for his continuing encouragement of my work.

Lee Edwards

Editor

CONTRIBUTORS

Clint Bolick is President and General Counsel of the newly formed School Choice Alliance and its companion organization, School Choice Advocates. He previously served as Vice President and co-founder of the Institute for Justice. A prolific author and frequent media commentator, Bolick is the author of *Leviathan: The Growth of Local Government and the Erosion of Liberty* (Hoover Institution Press).

Roger Clegg is Vice President and General Counsel of the Center for Equal Opportunity. A columnist for the *Legal Times*, Clegg held a number of positions at the Department of Justice, including Assistant to the Solicitor General and the number two official in the Civil Rights Division and the Environment Division.

John C. Eastman, a former law clerk to Supreme Court Justice Clarence Thomas, is Professor of Law at Chapman University School of Law and Director of the Claremont Institute Center for Constitutional Jurisprudence.

Lee Edwards is Distinguished Fellow for Conservative Thought at The Heritage Foundation and an Adjunct Professor of Politics at the Catholic University of America. He has published 15 books on American government and politics.

Thor L. Halvorssen was Executive Director and Chief Executive Officer of the Foundation for Individual Rights (FIRE) from its founding in 1999 until January 2004. He now serves as a member of FIRE's Board of Advisers.

David Kendrick directs the Organized Labor Accountability Project of the National Legal and Policy Center. He served as Legal Information Director of the National Right to Work Legal Defense Foundation from 1990–1994.

Mark R. Levin is President of the Landmark Legal Foundation. He held several top posts in the Reagan administration, including Chief of Staff to the Attorney General, Deputy Assistant Secretary for Elementary and Secondary Education at the Department of Education, and Deputy Solicitor at the Department of the Interior.

Edwin Meese III is Ronald Reagan Distinguished Fellow in Public Policy at The Heritage Foundation and Chairman of Heritage's Center for Legal and Judicial Studies. He served during the Reagan administration as the 75th Attorney General of the United States.

William H. "Chip" Mellor is President and General Counsel for the Institute for Justice, which he co-founded. He has written for such leading newspapers and journals as *The New York Times* and has appeared frequently on CBS, ABC, CNN, and other mass media.

Alan E. Sears is President, Chief Executive Officer, and General Counsel of the Alliance Defense Fund. He served under former Interior Secretary Don Hodel and as Executive Director of the Meese Commission on Pornography during the Reagan administration. He has trained hundreds of law enforcement officials from Australia to Scotland Yard.

Ronald A. Zumbrun co-founded the Pacific Legal Foundation and served as its initial Legal Director and then as its President and Chief Executive Officer for 22 years. Since 1995, he has headed the Zumbrun Law Firm, a prominent public issues law firm in Sacramento, California.